Just One More Song

**Conversations with My Wife
After Her Death**

Herbert Appleman

Library of Congress Control Number: 2019901651
ISBN: Hardcover   978-1-7960-1545-4
                 Softcover   978-1-7960-1544-7
                 eBook   978-1-7960-1543-0

Print information available on the last page.

From Hal Leonard LLC
Autumn Leaves
English lyric by Johnny Mercer
French lyric by Jacques Prevert
Music by Joseph Kosma
© 1947, 1950 (Renewed) ENOCH ET CIE
Sole Selling Agent for U.S. and Canada:
MORLEY MUSIC CO.,
By agreement with ENOCH ET CIE
All Rights Reserved
Reprinted by Permission of Hal Leonard LLC

From Birmingham Repertory Theatre, UK
Poster, A PERFECT GENTLEMAN
Copyright:
Birmingham Repertory Theatre, Birmingham, UK
Reproduced by kind permission.

From Alastair Muir & Regent's Park Open Air Theatre
Photo of Curtain Call, DAUNTLESS DICK DEADEYE
Copyright:
Alastair Muir & Regent's Park Open Air Theatre
Reproduced by kind permission.

Rev. date: 03/27/2019

To order additional copies of this book, contact:
Xlibris
1-888-795-4274
www.Xlibris.com
Orders@Xlibris.com
789454

Contents

Nearly every night before going to sleep, Dee liked me to sing to her. The song she'd pick would depend on her mood or the occasion, if the day was special, or simply on the time of year. On the first day of fall, when the colors began to change, she'd always pick "Autumn Leaves." More often than not, after I finished, she'd say, "Just one more song--this time you pick it."

For Dee
In Loving Memory

Prologue

Talking to Dee

As every writer knows, bad guys make fascinating characters. When they give in to temptation and break the rules and even the law, we join them vicariously but without any risk or guilt; we even get to feel morally superior.

Good guys, on the other hand, are a hard sell. We doubt anyone can be <u>that</u> good. "Come on," we say, "I'll bet that photo's been retouched."

It's a natural suspicion. I had it myself until I met Dee. Then slowly, over the years, I came to believe that just as Gershwin was a genius in music and Einstein in math and Michael Jordan in basketball, Dee was a genius in the art of living.

And, as it turned out, in the art of dying too.

Exhibit A: We were driving home to our house in Redding, Connecticut, after one of her last chemo treatments. Her CEA number had gone up, and things were getting scary. Suddenly, she smiled and said, "I want to give you a present." I asked her what the occasion was. "You are," she said. "I want you to know that I realize how hard it's been. I'm not only talking about the everyday stuff, though God knows there's been a ton of that-- driving me to work, picking me up for lunch, driving me to the hospital, thinking up interesting things to talk about during my chemo treatments..."

I tried to lighten the mood by saying I was beginning to think I was underpaid.

She chuckled, but her face remained serious. "What I'm really talking about is the <u>other</u> stuff. The way you've had to hide your own fears and pretend to be optimistic day after day without letup."

I thought I'd been subtle, but obviously I hadn't been subtle enough. Then she continued. "But look, it won't go on forever. Either I'll get better or—well, either way, you'll get a reprieve. And if the worst does happen—"

I put my finger to her lips. "Shhh . . ."

"I want you to remember—"

I shook my head. "I'm not listening."

"Please, Herb, let me say this. I want you to remember--this cancer is only supposed to kill one of us."

My conversations with Dee came about because I couldn't sleep. For a month or so after her death, I could only manage two or three hours of sleep a night. Even sleeping pills didn't help. Then, one night at around 4:00 a.m., I was stretched out on the sofa, trying to tire myself out by reading, when I suddenly remembered a scene from the movie *Sleepless in Seattle*. In this scene, Tom Hanks plays a character who's been recently widowed and is having trouble sleeping. Out of the blue, he imagines his dead wife sitting on the other end of the sofa, talking to him, and he feels comforted.

I thought I'd give it a try and imagined Dee sitting on the other end of the sofa.

She leaned forward and looked at me closely. "You look exhausted. Can't you sleep?"

"Not much," I said, then added, "I don't have an appetite either."

The symptoms, she thought, sounded familiar. "Maybe you're in love."

I agreed. "I guess that's the trade-off—the more you love someone, the sadder you are when that someone is gone."

She made the obvious joke: "We should've had a terrible marriage. Then you'd be happy now."

And I joked in return. "Isn't it lucky that I can be sad?"

She wasn't sure *lucky* was the right word, but she didn't know if there was a right word. Then she sighed. "I'm sorry. I thought you were ready."

I'd thought so too. But I guess death always takes you by surprise.

We sat quietly for a minute, then I began to unburden myself. "The hardest times are at night, when I reach out to hold you, and all that's there is an extra pillow. And in the morning, when I open my eyes and don't see your face."

She nodded. "I'd feel the same way."

Then I explained that once I got out of bed, the days were okay. I went to my desk, and there were a thousand things to take care of—the busy work connected with death. But as soon as night came...

She counseled me to give it time. "I've only been dead a month. It takes time for a scab to form."

"Who said anything about dead? As far as I'm concerned, you're at a meeting that's running late, but I'm expecting you back."

She smiled. "Well, here I am."

That first night, we talked for forty minutes. When the conversation was over, I fell asleep, quickly and naturally.

The next night, I talked to Dee again, with the same result. I wasn't afraid of the night anymore. In fact, I now looked forward to it. Instead of feeling her absence, I felt her presence--at least for a little while; and instead of struggling to fall asleep, all I had to do was say good night, blow her a kiss, and turn over.

I knew these conversations were imaginary; still, to me, they were as real as memory, imagination, and love are real. But I never felt there was anything mystical about them. At times I think we all hear voices in our heads—voices of parents, grandparents, teachers, friends, characters in literature, famous people we somehow feel close to, anyone we really love—voices that advise us or cheer us on or help us remember. Dee's voice did all that and more—it gave me the material for this book.

When I told our son, Marc, what I was writing about, he said, "You know, Dad, it's not just your gift to Mom--it's also her gift to you. She's the best subject you've ever had."

The First Year

August 25

Sooner Than Expected

On July 14, 1999, Dee had a hysterectomy. It was supposed to be a routine procedure. But during the operation, the surgeon discovered an advanced state of ovarian cancer.

Dee fought bravely for two years. She had a demanding job as executive director of A Child's Place, a day care/nursery school in Westport, Connecticut; but she never missed work, even when she had chemo treatments. On those days, I'd drive her to Columbia Presbyterian in upper Manhattan—she was always the last patient of the day—then back to Connecticut. By nine, she was asleep; by six the next morning, she was up and ready for another long day. She liked to be in her office by seven and be available to commuting parents who had to be on Metro-North by eight thirty.

But in June 2001, her body couldn't tolerate the chemo anymore. Throughout July, we crisscrossed the country looking for a nontoxic therapy, but we couldn't find one. Somehow, even then, she continued to work, but it was clear that she was going downhill.

Then on August 25, she decided it was time to have a just-in-case conversation.

It was sunset. We were sitting on a bench at her favorite spot in Westport, along Compo Beach, facing the Long Island Sound. She felt at home near the water, always had, ever since her childhood in Manhattan Beach, when the Atlantic Ocean was just a few steps from her front door.

She reached over and put her hand on mine. "We have to make some plans. Just in case."

I felt a shiver and said, "I'd rather not."

She understood but didn't think we had much choice.

I thought we did. "Look, I know what happened—a wave of sadness washed over you and knocked you down, but you'll get up again. You always do."

She put my hand to her cheek, held it there, then gathered herself together and turned to face me. "Look, I don't think I'm going to die tomorrow or next week or even next month. I still hope they'll come out with a new drug or I'll go into spontaneous remission or some kind of miracle will happen. But I'm a good administrator, and it makes sense to plan ahead just in case."

I knew what her plans were for and tried to postpone them, as if by doing so I could eliminate the need for them. "Why the hurry?"

Because, she explained, it wasn't something you could leave for the last second. "The last second always comes sooner than you expect it to."

There was no answer to that. "You're a brave girl."

She shrugged. "We're as brave as we have to be." And then she plunged in and told me her plans. First, she hated funeral parlors. She didn't think any building should be devoted entirely to death. She wanted the memorial service to be held at Temple Israel, where people were connected not only to death but also to weddings, bar mitzvahs, holidays, lectures, and concerts—the whole cycle of life; and where the setting was serene and beautiful, especially when the morning light poured through the windows.

I promised to arrange it.

Second, she didn't want to be buried—"It'd be like suffocating forever." Instead, she wanted to be cremated and have her ashes scattered in the Sound.

I was surprised. I'd assumed she'd want them scattered in the ocean, off the deck of the *Queen Elizabeth 2*.

Since 1976, I'd lectured many times on the *QE2*; my subject was American musical theater, and I'd talked about classic musicals in revival on Broadway or in the West End. We'd done transatlantic crossings, cruised the Mediterranean, and sailed on various legs of the round-the-world cruise. These trips ranked high among the special joys of our life, so naturally I assumed she'd want her ashes scattered in the ocean.

"No," she said, "I used to think that, but then I realized you'd have to keep them in the house until you sailed again, which might not be for months. And once on board, you'd be trying to enjoy yourself, but those damn ashes wouldn't let you."

I thanked her for the gallows humor.

"No, I think it's better to get it over with quickly. Besides, if you do it in Westport, you won't be alone. It'll be easier."

Her final instruction was about donations. If anyone wanted to make a donation in her name, they should send it to A Child's Place, where Frances and the board could use the money for a memorial fund to bring speakers to the school. "I always thought it was important to have at least one night a semester when parents, teachers, and administrators could get together to enjoy one another's company and be reminded that they were all on the same side." Then, ever practical, she added, "If there's a fund in place, my successor won't have to scrounge as I did to make up for the shortfall."

I promised her that I'd do everything she wanted.

Four days later, sooner than expected, she died.

August 29

Two Paintings I'll Never Sell

Dee was curious about every kind of experience. When she read Tolstoy's account of the day he sat at the bedside of his dying brother, she was fascinated. In writing about this scene, Tolstoy acknowledged that although one part of him was overwhelmed by sadness, another part was intensely interested in the sight of a man dying. To many readers, Tolstoy's reaction was monstrous, but Dee thought it was very human. So it wasn't hard for me to imagine that she'd want to know about her own death and that she'd say, "Look, Herb, dying was one of the big events of my life, and I missed it. Tell me what happened."

"You really want to know?"

"Yes."

It was Wednesday, the twenty-ninth. You woke up about six, as usual, and headed for the bathroom. Then I heard a loud thud; you must've tripped; and when I came in, your cheek was bleeding and your jaw was bruised. But nothing was broken. It didn't look too bad, and you still had a sense of humor. "Oh boy," you said, "bleeding . . . bald . . . some beauty . . ."

I helped you get up, and you leaned on me, and we slowly made our way back to bed. Once we got there, I tucked you in and said, "I'm going to call Dr. Tepler."

Suddenly, you were very quiet.

I touched you on the shoulder; when you didn't respond, I shook you gently. "Dee? Can you hear me?"

Quieter still.

I grabbed the phone and called 911. They answered on the first ring, asked a few questions, and immediately began to walk me through CPR.

I held you in my arms and breathed into your mouth.

Meanwhile, they contacted the West Redding Fire Station and the EMS ambulance in Danbury.

After just a few minutes, help arrived. But it was too late.

"I'm sorry," the person in charge said. "I think she's gone. We'll take her to the emergency room at Danbury Hospital, but I doubt if . . . I hope I'm wrong, but that's what I think."

"So," Dee interrupted, "I died in your arms, with your mouth on mine. I'm glad. That's more than I could've hoped for." Then she caught herself. "Forgive me, that's very selfish. It must've been awful for you."

"No," I said, "it seemed right."

"Okay, tell me the rest…"

I'd never been to Danbury Hospital before, and while driving there, my mind wasn't on the road, so I got a bit lost. By the time I reached the emergency room, you'd already been pronounced dead.

I was led to a curtained-off area where you were lying on a table.

I stood beside the table, alone with you, not thinking or even feeling anything, just numb.

Then Marc arrived, and we hugged and cried.

Then Dr. Tepler came, and he cried too.

We stayed there for another five minutes, staring at you. Or rather, at your body. Then it registered that the real you had already left. So we left too.

As I walked to my car, I tried to remember everything I could— your whole life—and drew a blank. The truth is, no one can remember a whole life or even a whole movie. It's too long and too complicated; we just remember a few images.

So, in the car, driving home, that's what I did—remembered a few images. I expected them to be faded images, like old snapshots, but they weren't. They were vivid, like scenes in HD.

First, there's a young girl of seventeen sitting on the rocks of the Esplanade, sketching—a really beautiful girl that I'm crazy about.

Then there's a college girl arriving in Boston for a weekend at Harvard. It's a crisp day in November. I'm waiting at the Back Bay station. The train pulls in, and people begin to get off. A familiar dot appears at the end of the platform. As it comes closer, I see a heart-shaped face framed by a fur hood and, below the hood, a long coat in a Russian Anna Karenina style. Suddenly, a sleeve trimmed with fur waves excitedly to get my attention. Then I hear you call, "Herb! Herb!" I wave back and call, "Dee! Over here!" Then we catch sight of each other, and it's like being in a Scott Fitzgerald story.

Then we're in my room in Adams House, lying in bed, and you're a Playboy centerfold come to life. My senses are extraordinarily alive, and I can smell at least five different scents: shampoo and soap and bath powder and Estee Lauder's White Linen, and headiest of all, you. Then, looking at your naked beauty and loving face and inviting arms, I suddenly get religion and can't help saying, "Thank You, God. Thank You, Thank You, Thank You."

Then there's the image of a smiling bride of twenty-one who could've been painted by Rembrandt. Then a radiant mother of twenty-two who could've been painted by Renoir--two paintings I'll never sell.

Then a brave and still-beautiful woman of sixty-seven who turns these last two years into the sweetest years of our life.

Dee shakes her head ruefully. "I wouldn't go that far."

I admit she has a point. "I'm not saying cancer was a plus. I'm just saying what happened to you was fate, but how you handled it—"

She insists she didn't always handle it as well as she should've. "There were times I cursed and cried my heart out."

"That's true," I say, "but only because I urged you to--because I thought you needed at least ten minutes a week when you could let your guard down. Hell, I even joined you."

"Yes, you did." She laughs. "That's what kept it to ten minutes. Once you joined me, the curses became funny."

Then her laugh trails off, and she says, "I'm sorry I made you go through that again—about my dying—but I really <u>did</u> want to know."

August 30

You Could Look It Up

In our next talk, I reported on how I'd carried out her instructions.

On Thursday morning, Marc and I went to the funeral parlor to arrange for the cremation. While there, we drafted a notice for the obituary column of the *New York Times*, and the funeral director phoned it in for us. The notice read as follows:

"Appleman, Dee. A woman of grace and beauty whose every breath was love."

Dee couldn't let that pass. "You painted with an awfully broad brush."

"No," I said, "those were the first words I thought of, and I thought of them because that's who you were."

"Really?" Then she reminded me that on two different occasions, we'd talked about divorce. "For only ten minutes each time, but still . . . And once, after we'd been married about eight years, we separated for a week, and you slept in your office on Seventy-Sixth Street."

"That doesn't count. It only shows we were human. And the proof is, I came home every night for dinner and talked with Marc until he went to bed. Then on one of those nights, it rained and I slept over and we made love and that was the end of our separation."

"Forgive me," Dee said. "I'm only trying to keep the memories real. If you turn me into Mary Noble, you'll forget who I really was."

I continued reading the notice. "Precious wife of Herb for forty-five years, mother of Marc, grandmother of Michael and Drew. Inspiring school director and teacher—"

"I hope so."

"Artist and author."

"A minor talent."

I disagreed. "A genuine talent that gave real pleasure—"

"To a small but loyal following."

Then I finished reading the notice. "Services Friday at 11:00 a.m. at Temple Israel, 14 Coleytown Road, Westport, Connecticut. Donations can be made to A Child's Place, Westport, in memory of Dee Appleman."

Dee was pleased. "Well done and not too flowery, except for 'whose every breath was love.'"

"I had to get *love* in there somewhere. I'm only sorry I didn't get *charming* in too."

"Was I that charming?"

"As Casey Stengel said, 'You could look it up.'"

Then her voice softened. "It must've been a hard day for you."

"It was hard for all of us."

That night, Marc was at his desk, writing, and I was at the kitchen table, writing. Michael looked in on us and wanted to know what we were doing. I told him we were preparing our remarks for Grandma Dee's memorial service the next morning. "What about me and Drew?" he asked. "Why aren't we preparing our remarks?"

I explained that since they were young—just eleven and eight—we thought it would be too hard for them to stand up in front of hundreds of people and talk about their sad feelings. Michael admitted it would be hard but argued, "It'll be just as hard for you and Dad, and you're doing it. I think we should do it too."

Drew agreed. "You know what Grandma Dee would say, 'You guys are terrific. You can do anything.'"

An hour later, they showed us what they'd written. This was Drew's speech (which Marc read at the service):

My Grandma Dee was very brave. When she was sick, she was still energetic, even though she didn't have any energy. She still did things with me, like having sleepovers, painting murals, playing cards, and even playing catch. I will always love her.

Dee was touched. "I'm glad the last thing I did with them just before they left on Tuesday was play catch on the lawn. I'm glad that's their last memory."

And this was Michael's speech:

To everyone out there who knew my Grandma Dee, you all know she was a wonderful person. She was also a wonderful grandma. She came to all my soccer and baseball games. She stood up for me when Mom and Dad got angry with me—even when she thought I was wrong. And she helped me out whenever I needed her. I will always have her in my heart.

Dee wasn't so sure. "For a while anyway. But I think memories of grandmas are like snow. After a storm, there are mountains of snow all over the ground. Kids think the snow will stay there forever. But eventually, the weather warms up, and one day, the snow is gone."

"But they'll always remember how beautiful it was."

"Maybe. In a blurry sort of way." She wasn't blaming them. "It's just how kids are. New memories come along, and the old ones melt away."

"Not for this kid," I said.

"Ah, but you were stuck on me."

August 31

Magical Changes

The memorial service was on Friday morning at Temple Israel, as Dee had requested. The temple windows, made of clear glass, reached from floor to ceiling. Now, as if on cue, the light poured through them.

I was the first speaker. I talked about our visit to Dr. Herbert Benson, a pioneer in the field of mind-body medicine. Dr. Benson guided us through a labyrinth of memories and then, meeting with each of us separately, helped us choose our mantras. Independently, we both chose the same word, *ocean*. He was stunned. "I've been doing this a long time," he said, "but until now, I've never had a couple who chose the same mantra. I think you two should get married."

And then, at the end, I fell back on a cliché. I tried to think of something original, but I kept coming back to the image of light.

I turned my head to look through the windows and said, "I can see that it's light out, but I don't believe it. If Dee is gone, how can there be light? The only explanation I can think of is that so many people have memories of Dee, and these memories are so bright--they continue to light the world."

Dee told me not to worry about the cliché. Even God used it. To start the universe, all He could think of was "Let there be light." I was in good company.

"Speaking of company," I said, "you drew quite a crowd. Over two hundred. There would've been even more, but this was just before the Labor Day weekend. And a lot of people in Manhattan and Westport were away. Even so, a good many came back early so they could be at the service."

"I was a real nuisance, wasn't I?"

"Yes," I said, "it was very inconsiderate of you to die just before Labor Day."

Then I told her about the other speakers: Marc and Michael; Lin, Keren, and Mia; Judy and Frances.

"Why so many?"

"I couldn't keep them away."

Marc began by saying, "She was the best," and that was the phrase everyone quoted afterward. Then he went on to list special moments the two of you had shared, ending with the daily walks you took through the construction site as their house was being built.

Lin spoke about how you were the sister she'd always wanted; and Keren and Mia, speaking separately, made the same point: that you always made them feel good about themselves.

Judy, who'd known you since you were teenagers, said that through all those years, there was one constant: whether she was down at the beach with you sketching or just walking and talking, "being with Dee was a holiday."

Finally, Frances talked about how you transformed A Child's Place. "Dee convinced us that people need light and color and beauty to learn and grow, and she led us to make magical changes to the school. Today, A Child's Place sparkles, and what it sparkles with is Dee's spirit."

Dee observed wryly that people got carried away, but I said, "No, they just told the truth. As I wrote in the obits that ran in the Westport and Redding papers, you were someone who changed hundreds of lives."

She blushed a little, then said, "For that, kind sir, much thanks."

September 3

Dee as Dear Abby

When I wrote that Dee had changed hundreds of lives, I wasn't exaggerating. Proof came in this morning's mail, which included twelve letters of condolence—two of them from young women who'd been teachers under Dee at Berkeley Carroll and A Child's Place. These women had turned to Dee in moments of crisis and confusion because they had misgivings about the men they were engaged to marry.

Here, sufficiently altered to protect the privacy of the couples, are their stories (as Dee told them to me at the time they happened).

Katy said she really liked Jim, and because he'd had such a hard time as a child, she felt enormous pity for him. But she wasn't madly in love with him and wondered if that was important or even realistic.

I was tempted to tell her that playing Dear Abby was beyond my pay grade, but she was so distraught, I decided to risk a few words of general advice. "Look," I said, "the way I see it, pity isn't a good basis for marriage. It leads to self-sacrifice, and sooner or later, self-sacrifice leads to resentment. What you should be looking for, in my opinion, is a man you admire, who excites you as a lover, shares your values and interests as a friend, and is someone you really like to talk to."

My words must've made sense to her because she didn't marry Jim. Instead, she went looking for the kind of man I'd described.

Two years later, she found him.

The problem facing the second teacher was different.

Lillian was already engaged to Trevor, but she was still trying to decide if he had all the qualities she wanted in a husband. She showed me a list of twenty qualities she felt were essential, then asked me what I thought.

I read the list, turned the page over, saw it was blank, and asked her where Trevor's list was.

She said Trevor didn't have a list.

I said that didn't seem fair.

Then she asked me whose side I was on.

I said I was on both sides.

At first she felt betrayed, but then she saw what I was driving at.

The next time they met, she asked Trevor for his list.

He was bowled over! It changed their relationship and really helped them get to know each other and learn to love each other, and eventually to get married.

After Lillian left teaching, she still kept in touch with Dee. Whenever she had a problem, Dee was the first person she turned to. One time, when she called, I picked up the phone.

Dee had given her good advice again, and she wanted to thank her.

I said I'd pass her thanks along.

"There's something else you can pass along," she said with an unmistakable smile in her voice. "The worst-kept secret of the faculty lounge."

"What's that?"

"Every woman on her staff wanted to be just like her."

September 4

It Isn't So Easy to Scatter Ashes

Marc and I thought we'd go out at sunset and scatter Dee's ashes off the jetty in Westport, but we did a dry run first. Which was lucky because the jetty was crowded and noisy.

Then we tried Burying Hill--not just because of the name but because it was out of the way and likely to have the quiet and privacy we wanted. But it didn't. Obviously, sunset is a popular time for people to stroll or sit by the water.

That's when I realized we'd have to get a boat and sail far from shore.

So I called our friends Rebecca and Olav and asked them if they'd be willing to take us out on <u>their</u> boat. They said they'd be honored, and since their boat was quite large, they invited me to invite other guests.

September 6

Sunset

Two nights later, at sunset, we left the marina in Norwalk, sailed far out into the Sound, and finally anchored off the Westport shore. In addition to Rebecca and Olav, the group included most of the people who'd spoken at Dee's memorial service.

It was a gorgeous evening. The sky was covered with a wash of pale orange and violet that looked like the background of a watercolor that Dee might've painted.

Despite the fact that her ashes were on deck, there was nothing morbid about the occasion. It had the feeling of a quiet party. We talked about Dee. We toasted her. And then I said, "We're here to carry out Dee's last wish. Some of her happiest days and nights were spent sailing the ocean on the *QE2*. Her mantra word was *ocean*, and now her ashes will become part of the ocean. In Jewish tradition, each mourner at the graveside is invited to throw some earth on the casket. In the spirit of that tradition, I invite each of you to scatter some of Dee's ashes into the ocean."

When I told Dee about the ceremony on the boat, she thought it sounded lovely; then, before I dropped off to sleep, she said, "That's enough about death. Let's plan to talk about something else tomorrow. Something that's fun."

I knew exactly what it should be.

I explained that, recently, I'd been dreaming about our first date. I mentioned this to Joe Schildkraut. Joe was a psychiatrist and my oldest friend. In kindergarten, we'd competed for the job of class monitor. At Harvard, we'd been roommates. And in the years since, we'd kept in close touch even when separated by a continent or an ocean. "What do you think it means?" I asked. "Why should I suddenly dream about that first date?"

He didn't have an answer, at least not as a psychiatrist; but as a friend, he said, "You know how you feel after you finish a wonderful book—you want to go back to the beginning and start all over again."

Dee smiled. "I always knew he was an old softie."

"Okay then," I said, "tomorrow we'll go on our first date again."

The only thing wrong with these talks is that I can't wait to get through the day so that we can talk again.

September 7

First Date

Dee and I met when we were students at Lincoln High School in Brooklyn, New York, but we didn't date then. During our high school years, I was busy dating older girls from the varsity drama club. It wasn't until early September, before my sophomore year at Harvard and Dee's freshman year at Syracuse, that we had our first date.

I'd just come home after a season as dramatics counselor at a summer camp. I called up two of the older girls from the varsity club, but they were still out of town, away at jobs or traveling. So I took out my little notepad filled with names and phone numbers. Under *Cargoes,* I came across Dee's name. *Cargoes* was the school magazine where I'd been a literary editor and Dee had been an art editor. As I continued leafing through the notepad, I came across her name on two other pages. Then I remembered why she was worth so many entries: she was very talented. The first painting of hers I'd ever seen, *Circus Clown,* which was done when she was sixteen, impressed me very much. (And still does.) She also had a lovely face, a knock-out figure, and a contagious smile that made <u>you</u> smile.

I decided to call her.

Circus Clown

"Dee? It's Herb. Herb Appleman."

There was a pause, then a chuckle. "I've been waiting for you to call for a whole year. What took you so long?"

"I've <u>been</u> calling. The line was always busy."

She wasn't convinced. "For a whole year?"

"You're very popular."

"With everyone but you."

I pleaded guilty. "My mistake, which I'd like to correct. Any chance you're free tonight?"

There was another pause, followed by another chuckle. "I <u>should</u> say no. This is very last minute. But the fact is, I <u>am</u> free. And if I don't say yes, I may have to wait <u>another</u> year."

I promised that she wouldn't. "But I'm glad you said yes. I'll borrow my father's car and pick you up after dinner. Seven, okay?"

"Seven's fine."

Then we did the usual first-date thing and went to a movie. We chose *The Quiet Man*, a romantic comedy with John Wayne and Maureen O'Hara. It turned out to be really good and made us feel that everything about this first date was going right.

As we sat in the balcony, I struggled with the classic dating dilemma: should I put my arm around Dee, or should I just hold her hand? I decided to be patient and mature, and I just held her hand. It was the only time I was ever shy with her.

After the movie, we went to a diner and had coffee and pie. Then we drove to the beach and walked along the Esplanade. There was a half moon, so I began to sing.

> *Moonlight becomes you,*
> *It goes with your hair,*
> *You certainly know the right things to wear.*
> *Moonlight becomes you so.*

Dee applauded politely.

"Didn't you like it?"

"Well," she said, trying to let me down gently, "it's kind of corny."

I was deflated. "Oh. Sorry."

"No." She laughed. "I was just teasing! Really! No one ever sang to me before. It's very romantic. Please sing some more."

"You're sure?"

"Absolutely."

So I sang the bridge, then when I got to the final stanza, I put aside the real lyrics and made up my own.

> *Does this mean I love you?*
> *It's too soon to know . . .*
> *Besides which, it's very corny...*

And to my surprise, Dee finished up with,

> *Although,*
> *I'd like to think it's so.*

"You would?" I asked.

"Don't panic." She laughed. "We're just kidding around, just flirting."

I wasn't so sure. "You're very special. This whole night is special."

She nodded. "I thought it would be."

"Why didn't you get me to call you sooner?"

"You weren't ready," she said, then added dryly, "You were going through an 'older woman' phase."

We talked for at least an hour more, then I walked her home. At her door, we kissed for the first time.

"It was a long kiss," Dee remembered, "and it actually made me dizzy. When it was over, I went inside the house and closed the door and thought to myself, *You know what the Italian girls from Coney Island would say—'You've been hit by the thunderbolt!'*"

Actually, there were two thunderbolts that night.

31

September 17

Second Thoughts

During the next week, I notified the insurance company, filed a claim at the Social Security office, donated our second car to the Guild for the Blind, and met with lawyers to have Dee's will probated and my will revised.

But I did these things on automatic pilot. My head was elsewhere, thinking about the possibility of an afterlife.

Up till now, I'd never believed in one. As I saw it, the best we could hope for was that we'd live on in the memories of those who loved us and that our works, if they were still valued, would live on in the minds of others.

But now that Dee was dead, I was having second thoughts.

I rejected the atheist view that the universe just happened to happen and when you die, you're dead forever. I suppose, in our present state of knowledge, that's as close to the factual truth as we can get. But if you're in mourning for someone you loved, and still love, that knowledge offers little comfort. Only the idea of an immortal soul offers real comfort and satisfies the imagination.

But unfortunately, the idea of a soul, immortal or otherwise, isn't quite respectable nowadays. At least among intellectuals. Most of them don't even consider it an idea—just a hope, an unscientific hope, inspired by faith.

It was in this mood of perplexity that I went to see the rabbi who'd conducted Dee's memorial service.

When I asked him about the Jewish view of the afterlife, he told me there were two views. "For Orthodox Jews, belief in the World to Come is mandatory. Unless goodness is finally rewarded and evil is finally punished, there's no justice in the universe. And if there's no justice, there's no God."

I responded that the logic was sound, but unfortunately, there was no evidence to back it up. He was forced to agree. "That's why in the Reform tradition, we take a different view. To us, the Orthodox view is appealing, but what it proves is not that the World to Come exists but that God has given us a <u>desire</u> for such a world—a world where justice is finally and perfectly done and where some part of us, some indefinable part that we call the soul, lives on. As we say in the Yom Kippur service, 'God has put eternity into our hearts and implanted within us a vision of life everlasting.'"

I asked him to be more specific, but he said there were no specifics.

I mentioned that I'd always heard God was in the details, but he parried, "Not when it comes to eternity." Then his voice softened. "But we're not really talking about eternity, are we? We're talking about grief. And when it comes to grief, I'm inclined to let people find comfort wherever they can. So if it gives you comfort to imagine an afterlife, by all means, imagine it. But not too often. Don't make it your home. While you're alive, your primary residence is here on earth, and your primary connection is to the living."

After I shared this conversation with Dee, she said, "He's right."

I knew that; it made sense. The only trouble is, death doesn't put you in a sensible frame of mind. Then it occurred to me that I shouldn't be telling Dee about the afterlife, <u>she</u> should be telling me.

"I can't," she said. "Remember, you're making up both parts of this conversation. All I can tell you is what you already know."

"Damn! I was hoping for a breakthrough—a message from the other side."

"No such luck." Then she perked up. "But all is not lost. I <u>can</u> tell you what heaven is like. I've known since I was a young girl. It's a place where the season is always autumn and you have to wear a sweater and every house on the block has a fireplace and the air smells of burning wood and every leaf is like a flower."

"Nice," I said, "but I want a place where you're still alive."

"Me too. Give me the address, and I'll come right over."

September 20

When a Book Really Moves You

Helen Stauderman was the head librarian at the Mark Twain Library in Redding. For the last three years, I'd hosted a film series at the library, and Helen had become our friend. Now she called to say, "You know how much I liked Dee and admired her as an artist. What would you think of my putting up a memorial exhibit in the library?"

I said I thought that would be lovely and, the next day, brought over a representative selection of Dee's paintings and illustrations, including two favorites of mine, *Garden of Eden* and *A Flower in my Sketchbook*. Then over a cup of coffee, Helen asked me about Dee's career so she'd know what to write on the cards in the display cases.

I gave her a thumbnail sketch:

Dee showed talent early. While still in elementary school, she was invited to take art lessons every Saturday morning at the Brooklyn Museum. In high school, she became one of the art editors of Cargoes, won citywide competitions, and ultimately won art scholarships to Cooper Union and Syracuse. Because she wanted to go out of town, she chose Syracuse.

Garden of Eden

A Flower in my Sketchbook.

After Syracuse, she worked as a freelance artist—at first full-time, but soon only part-time during summers and Christmas vacations. She did watercolors for greeting cards and illustrated six books, including <u>When Two Become Three</u>, a memoir I wrote about the difference a child makes in the life of a young couple.

Helen was confused. "Back up a second. Why only during summers and Christmas vacations?"

Because, I explained, after Marc was born, I gave up freelancing as a writer and went to work in television, doing documentaries; and Dee gave up freelancing as an artist and switched careers from art to education—partly because she thought one of us should have a secure job with a reliable income, and partly because she realized that she liked to work with people and felt she had a gift for bringing out the best in them.

Teaching was an obvious choice, especially since the short teaching day gave her enough time to be a hands-on wife and mother, and that was always her priority.

In time, she became an extraordinary teacher, not only of children but of student teachers. She mentored them in her classroom; and with her colleague, Johanna McClear, she wrote <u>Teacher, The Children Are Here</u>, an informal textbook that was used in teacher ed courses for many years. Eventually, she became a headmistress: first at the Berkeley Carroll Elementary School in Brooklyn, then at the Wilson Elementary School in New Jersey, and finally, at A Child's Place in Westport.

"Did she have any regrets," Helen wondered, "at switching from art to education?"

"No. And she never thought of it as a sacrifice. To her, it was a choice—a good choice that benefited her family, enlarged her life, and gave her a chance to develop other sides of her nature."

Helen had one last question. "I need an anecdote to make the facts come alive. Can you remember something that happened that made you realize for the first time how special Dee was?"

I smiled. "That's easy. It was the first time she visited me at Harvard."

We were having dinner at the Henri Quatre restaurant in Cambridge. As we waited for dessert, I took out a gift-wrapped book from my reading bag and handed it to her. It was a book that I'd just read for a course on the immigrant in American history. "It's called *The Uprooted*," I said. "And it's by Oscar Handlin, the professor who teaches the course. It's very personal, not at all like a textbook. A lot of the time, it quotes from letters and diaries to let the immigrants tell the story in their own words."

Dee thanked me and said she'd read it on the train.

I predicted that she'd probably finish it before she got to Syracuse. "It reads like the wind--I read it in one night."

Then she asked me a question that no one had ever asked me before. "Now that you've had this experience, what are you going to do with it?"

I asked her what she meant. "What does anyone do with a book he reads? I'll store it in my memory, then refer to it when the subject comes up."

"No," she said, "that's what you do with an ordinary book. But when you read something that really moves you, it's not enough to file it away. You have to <u>act</u> on it."

I was lost. "Act how?"

"That depends on what moved you."

I explained that I was moved because it was the story of my parents. Because Handlin had brought home to me just how painful their uprooting had been, how much courage it had taken for them to start over—without knowing the language, without having an education, without having a job. I really felt for them and was very proud of them.

"Did you tell them that?" she asked. "Did you call home and tell them?"

"Not yet."

"You should," she said. "Better still, you should write them a letter, then they'll have it always and be able to read it over and over."

"I suppose . . ."

She reached across the table to touch my hand. "It'll mean a lot to them. Not only because it'll show that you appreciate what they had to go through, but because it'll prove that they don't have to be afraid of Harvard-- that it won't take you away from them."

I wrote the letter, and it worked exactly as she'd predicted.

September 21

"Autumn Leaves"

Today is the first day of fall, and as I noted in my dedication, that's when Dee always asked me to sing "Autumn Leaves."

One year, I serenaded her in Central Park. The air was crisp, and the park was ablaze with a dozen shades of green, yellow, red, and maple. As we walked, arm in arm, on a path overlooking the lake, Dee leaned her head against my shoulder; I sang, and she hummed along.

After I finished singing, we stopped and sat on the grass. Then she had a favor to ask. "I want you to put on your professor's hat and help me out. I'm not sure I understand that lyric. It's very evocative, but what does it mean?"

It was always great fun to teach Dee. She was the best—and most beautiful—student I ever had. "Okay," I said, "let's take a close look. And before we get to the lyric, let's set the scene."

She smiled knowingly because I was doing what she'd taught me to do: make the first question easy to give the student confidence. "Okay," she said, "the time is obviously autumn, and the place is a room with a window, and the window looks out on a yard covered with leaves." Then she sketched in the rest of the room. "A young man is sitting at a desk, writing a letter to a young woman with whom he recently had a summer romance—"

"And," I chimed in, "because he calls her 'my darling' at the end of the letter, I think it's safe to say that's how he begins."

Dee nodded, said, "My darling," and paused. "Then what?"

"He's not sure. He has trouble finding the right words. So he looks out the window for inspiration—"

"And sees the leaves drifting by—"

"And <u>finds</u> the right words."

Softly, reflectively, she sang the first stanza.

The falling leaves drift by the window,
The autumn leaves of red and gold.
I see your lips—the summer kisses—
The sunburned hands I used to hold.

"There," she said, "right at the beginning, even those lines give me trouble."

I thought I knew why. "It's because the first two lines are about leaves, but the next two are about memories. When he sees the red leaves, he remembers her red lips and their kisses. He calls them summer kisses, not only because that's <u>when</u> he kissed her, but—?" I let the question hang.

"Because their kisses were so warm—"

"And when he sees the gold leaves, he remembers not only her tan—"

Anticipating my next question, she finished the sentence. "But the burning excitement he felt when he held her hand."

I nodded, and she went on to sing the bridge.

Since you went away, the days grow long,
And soon I'll hear old winter's song.

"Okay," I said, "this part is a little tricky. The fact is, in autumn, the days grow shorter. But for him, since she went away, the time is empty—"

"So they <u>feel</u> longer—"

"And then he has a sudden premonition—"

"That he may never see her again, and all he'll have left when he gets old and reaches the winter of life—"

"Is the faint song of memory."

She picked a leaf off the grass and twirled it thoughtfully between her fingers. "I was right—this isn't a simple lyric."

Then she sang the coda.

> *But I miss you most of all, my darling,*
> *When autumn leaves start to fall.*

"And now," I said, "we know why the song is called 'Autumn Leaves.' Because even if the memories of that summer grow fainter with the passing years—"

"They'll always come back to him—"

"Every autumn—"

"When the leaves of memory drift by his window."

Then she gave a big smile and clapped her hands. "That's for you—and Johnny Mercer. He managed to get an awful lot into those few lines, didn't he?"

"Yes, he did."

As we got up, she stood on tiptoe and kissed me. "Thanks, Prof!"

Then we resumed our walk, and she said, as I knew she would, "Just one more song-- this time you pick it."

September 29

Watch Out for Happiness

It was now a month since Dee had died, and I was trying to pick up the pieces of everyday life. And so this afternoon, I went to Michael's soccer game.

Michael was an exceptional athlete, good at every sport, and particularly good at soccer, where his speed, dribbling skill, and ability to kick the ball hard with either leg made him a standout. Today, he was in the zone and wound up scoring four goals—his highest total ever, in his best game ever.

As I drove back to Redding, I was beaming. It had been a memorable day, and I was glad I'd been there to hear all his teammates and their parents cheer, "Mi-chael! Mi-chael!"

But when I opened the door to my house, something unexpected happened—I was suddenly overcome by sadness. And I couldn't understand why. Then it hit me: happiness wants to be shared, and if the person you've always shared it with isn't there, it turns into sadness.

So how, I wondered, can you protect yourself?

"Well," Dee said, "obviously, you don't want to avoid happiness. You just want to avoid the letdown afterward. So next time you're feeling happy, stop for a second and remind yourself to watch out for the letdown."

It was uncanny. The answers she gave me were answers I already knew, but somehow they didn't register until I imagined her saying them. Then she asked if she could tell me something else I already knew.

"Go ahead."

"I think there's another reason you felt sad when you came home. I think it's because this house is spooky—the place where I died."

"But that only took a minute," I said. "To me, it's where you lived."

She still thought it was spooky and felt I'd be better off in Westport, near Marc and the boys. "Maybe you could find a carriage house—"

I explained that even if I wanted to, I didn't have the strength to look for a place and pack and move and unpack. I just wasn't up to it.

"Forgive me," she said, "you're still running on fumes." Then she changed the subject and thanked me for telling her about Michael.

"Next time," I promised, "I'll bring you up to date on Drew."

October 5

Sleepover

During the last few years, Dee and I had taken one of the boys for a sleepover every Friday night. We began by taking both of them in order to give their parents a night off, but we soon learned that two brothers on a sleepover was one brother too many. To avoid sibling rivalry and grievous bodily harm, we alternated our invitations, taking Michael one week and Drew the next, thereby giving each one the benefit of undivided attention.

Tonight, the first sleepover since Dee's death, was Drew's turn. I picked him up in Westport, and we set out on the twenty-five-minute drive to Redding. He was only eight and, under Connecticut law, had to sit in the back seat. Even though we weren't face-to-face, drive time was a good time to talk, and we usually had a lively conversation. But not tonight.

"How come?" Dee wondered.

I said I didn't know. "Maybe he felt funny, knowing you wouldn't be at the house. Whatever the reason, it was a very quiet drive. We managed a few words about the Yankees and the new Harry Potter book, but after that, nothing. Finally, I said, 'C'mon, Drew, there must be <u>something</u> we can talk about.' Reluctantly, pushed to the wall, he asked me, 'So, Grandpa, how are you doing in school?'"

Dee burst out laughing.

"Wait!" I said, "that's not the end. Because he was sitting in back, he didn't see me smile and must've thought his wit was too subtle for me. So he tapped me on the shoulder and asked, 'Do you get it?' That did it. I laughed so hard I had to pull off the road!"

Then I quickly described the rest of the night. "When we got to the house, we had dinner, then played poker and Jotto, a word game Drew loved and was very good at. Around eight, we got into bed and began to watch an old movie. But after about ten minutes, Drew fell asleep, so I turned the video off and saved the movie for the morning."

Dee was envious. "My favorite kind of sleepover—an ordinary night when everything seems special."

October 6

A Proposal

When Marc was a young boy, I didn't want him to miss out on the old movies of Errol Flynn and Tyrone Power—adventure classics that I'd seen and loved when I was his age. Since there were no videos then, I took him on Saturday morning excursions to the only places where those movies were shown: the Museum of Modern Art, the Huntington Hartford Museum at Columbus Circle, and the New Yorker movie theater on Broadway.

None of his friends had ever heard of Errol Flynn and Tyrone Power, but Marc soon knew all their movies: *The Sea Hawk*, *Captain Blood*, *The Adventures of Robin Hood*, *The Mark of Zorro*...

By the time Michael and Drew became old enough to watch movies, the situation had greatly improved. Nearly all those movies were now on videos that could be played at home, either rented from Blockbuster or borrowed from the library.

This morning, Drew and I were watching *Captain Blood*. It starred Flynn and Olivia de Havilland. As always, when I saw Olivia de Havilland, I thought of Dee. The resemblance was striking: the heart-shaped face, the gentle voice, the unforced charm. In *Captain Blood*, Olivia de Havilland looked very young—as young as Dee on the day I proposed.

It was the first day of spring break in our senior year. We were walking on the Esplanade. I stopped and took her hand. "Listen," I said, "I know we're too young to get married, but if we don't do it now, months will go by—maybe years—and we'll risk losing each other. And if that ever happened, I'd—"

Before I could finish, she threw her arms around my neck. "So would I." We kissed until we were breathless.

Coming up for air, I said, "I thank God every day for giving you to me."

"Oh, Herb, I thank Him too."

Then I took a step back and announced very seriously. "But I can't let you accept my proposal until you hear me out." She was suddenly worried and wanted to know what was wrong.

I paused to collect my thoughts; in a voice that was uncharacteristically hesitant, I began to explain that there was something I had to tell her, something that might change her mind. I hoped it wouldn't, but it was something she'd have to think about and probably discuss with her parents.

Dee became pale. "What is it?"

After hiding the secret from her for three years, I let it out. "It's my mother. She suffers from depression. It's been going on for a long time—since I was a kid. Almost every year, she has a breakdown and has to be hospitalized." As earthquakes go, I figured that was a five on the Richter scale. "I'm very involved. She hates the hospital and won't sign herself in unless I promise to stay with her during the shock treatments. If we were married, you'd be involved too. It's a lot to take on."

Dee was stunned. Who wouldn't be? But even in that first moment, her astonishment was already mixed with concern. "Why didn't you tell me before?"

"I was a coward," I said, then added, in my own defense. "No, that's not true or, anyway, not the whole truth. I <u>couldn't</u> tell you because it's a family secret. Actually, it's a family shame. No one's supposed to know. But just now, I decided <u>you</u> had to." And then I stated the facts as objectively as I could. "There are two issues: the burden of my mother and genetics. You might not want to take a chance on having children who—"

Dee interrupted. "But you and your sister are okay."

"We seem to be. Still, you might not like the odds."

"Look," she said, "genetics is always a risk. For everyone." Then she put her hand on my cheek. "You've been carrying a heavy load all by yourself. I'd like to help."

Incredibly, my parents had refused to meet Dee. They thought we were getting too serious and didn't want to encourage us. "You want to be a writer," they said. "She wants to be an artist. When you graduate, you should concentrate on your careers. You shouldn't be tied up in marriage."

When I told them at dinner that I'd proposed and that Dee had accepted, they were very upset, especially my father. "Four years at Harvard, and he still doesn't know the first thing about life."

Then my mother became agitated. "What about my condition? Did you tell her?"

"I told her," I said. "And she wants to help."

My mother looked down at her lap. "She'll think I'm a crazy woman."

"No, she won't," I said. "She'll think you've had a lot of pain in your life. She'll be sympathetic."

Then my father sighed dramatically. "All right, it can't be put off any longer. We'll have to meet her. All right, bring her over tomorrow afternoon. We'll have tea and cookies."

And so Dee came over the next afternoon and sat in the witness box. Now it was _my_ turn to be agitated. But, really, there was no need. She made an excellent witness. She wasn't at all nervous or self-conscious. She was just herself, and put everyone at ease.

After ten minutes, my father suddenly stood up and announced, "I was wrong. You two should get married. It would be a crime if you didn't. You'd never forgive yourselves." Then he turned to me and said, "You were right. She's beautiful, she's an artist, she loves you, she's a very nice person, and she's Jewish. You couldn't do better if you looked a hundred years."

My mother agreed.

"And from that moment," Dee said, "she called me Deedarling, as if it were one word."

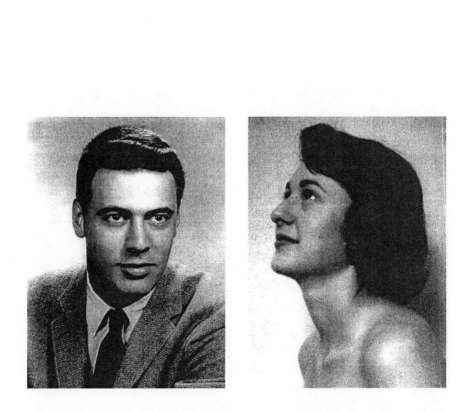

At the time of our engagement

October 8

Anticipating Change

We were married in 1955, shortly after our graduation from college. We were both twenty-one. Eight months later, a frog told Dee she was pregnant. It wasn't something we'd planned on, but Dee embraced the news. She was never fazed by the prospect of change. She was always ready to take the next step in her life; she had a rare ability to disarm change by anticipating it. It was a strategy she'd learned at an early age from her mother.

I first heard about this strategy one night when she was in her sixth month. We were lying in bed, in our favorite spoon position, with my free hand cupping her breast, when she gently moved my hand away, kissed it, then turned to face me. "You know," she said, "a baby will mean the end of our first marriage."

I gave her a puzzled look.

"For an entire year," she explained, "we've been on an extended honeymoon. Every night, we've stayed up late to read or watch TV or listen to music or make love. On Sunday mornings, we stayed in bed till noon."

"Sounds good to me."

"It was! It was wonderful! But once the baby comes, it'll have to end. Because a baby doesn't come by itself, it brings all sorts of changes with it. And if we're not ready for those changes, we'll be overwhelmed by them, and pretty soon we'll resent the baby, and then we'll resent each other."

"I've heard happier scenarios."

Then she explained that if we learned to plan ahead, we could still do everything we liked—only not as often and not as spontaneously, but even more joyously because we'd have a baby! And we'd be off on a new adventure—our second marriage."

I looked confused again. "What're you talking about?"

"The way I see it, a couple who stays married for a lifetime has at least seven different marriages."

"Only seven?"

"I said at least!"

Then she ran down the list:

1. Extended honeymoon
2. First child
3. Focus on husband's career
4. Focus on wife's return to work
5. Midlife crisis
6. Empty nest
7. Retirement

"Of course," she added, "there can be more than seven, if there are more children or there's a catastrophic illness or—"

"In other words," I said, "a marriage that lasts a lifetime can wind up being a dozen marriages."

"Or more! And that's a good thing! Otherwise, a couple who stayed married for a lifetime would die of boredom!"

I stared at her in wonder. "You're only twenty-two. How do you know all this?"

"I've known it since I was twelve." And then she explained. "On my twelfth birthday, my mother sat me down and talked to me about my first period, which she was sure I'd be getting very soon. She warned me it would be uncomfortable and I'd definitely have some bleeding. Then she patted my hand. 'But don't worry, it sounds worse than it is. The important thing is, the day it happens will mark a turning point in your life.'"

And then Dee told the rest of the story in her mother's Southern accent. (Her mother, whose name was Rounette Belle, had been born and raised in South Carolina.) "'It will turn you,' my mother continued, 'in the direction of becoming a woman. And soon the little rosebuds on your chest will bloom, and the sharp angles of your body will soften, and the young men will not be able to leave you alone. The phone will ring, the doorbell will ring, the very air will ring because as all the world knows, looks come first with a man. And you, thank God, are as pretty as Charleston in the spring.'

"And then my mother spoke about the years just ahead, the years in high school and college—years filled with books to read and courses to take and football games on Saturday afternoons, and parties and dances on Saturday nights, and trips to Manhattan.

"And then she shifted into high gear. 'And there will be all kinds of romances, and from these romances, you will find out about young men and about yourself, and then you'll be able to choose wisely when it's time to marry.

"And after you marry, if fate is kind, you'll become a mother. And nothing is more important than that. Because the human race has to be born again in every generation, and mothers do the bearing.

"'Of course,' she was quick to add, 'since you have a talent for art and get straight A's, you will also play other roles in life. But mind that word also, because nothing will fill your heart like being a wife and mother.'

Then she held out her arms and hugged me. 'And just think, all these wonderful things will begin to happen as soon as you get your first period!'"

"I could hardly wait!"

"Meanwhile," Dee concluded, "other girls I knew who hadn't been prepared by a mother like mine were traumatized by their first period and had an extremely painful time of it, and continued to have painful periods for years to come. What's even sadder was that the whole idea of sex became associated in their minds with dirtiness and suffering.

"But I was lucky. On that day, I learned the great lesson that certain changes are natural and inevitable, and whether they turn out to be wonderful or horrible depends on how you prepare for them."

HERBERT APPLEMAN

When Two Become Three

Illustrated by DEE APPLEMAN

October 11

See It Every Day

Since Dee's memorial service and her obituary notice in the *New York Times*, Marc and I had received over two hundred letters and cards of condolence from relatives, friends, and colleagues. I tried to answer each letter with a handwritten personal note, but after a while, my hand became sore, and I ran out of emotional energy.

Marc and I talked it over and decided to have our acknowledgment cards printed. But when I proofed the cards, I realized that a printed card is a plain dish. We needed something to go with it. Then I had a brain wave and knew what that something should be: one of the watercolor sketches from Dee's Jerusalem sketchbook.

In 1991, Dee and I had been guests of the city of Jerusalem and were invited to stay in a small villa at the Mishkenot Sha'ananim—a group of villas that had been built to house distinguished artists and scholars from abroad. The first guests had been megastars like Arthur Rubinstein, Isaac Stern, Leonard Bernstein, and Saul Bellow.

Obviously, Dee and I were lesser lights who'd gotten in on a pass. We stayed at the Mishkenot for a month and had a marvelous time. As we roamed through the city, Dee filled her sketchbook with more than twenty watercolor sketches—small sketches but so beautiful that when we got back to New York, I had five of them printed as greeting cards.

"Which sketch did you pick?" Dee asked.

"*Walls of the Old City.*"

"I hope they liked it."

"I have a stack of thank-you notes that says they did. In fact, most of them said they framed the sketch and put it in their kitchen, where they could see it every day."

Walls of the Old City

October 18

Matching Clothes and Friends

Dee's jewelry box and closets full of clothes kept staring at me. I knew I had to dispose of them, but something held me back. They were the last tangible reminders of how she'd looked. It was comforting to have them around. And then I remembered that they weren't relics. According to Jewish tradition, I had an obligation to restore them to the world so that other women could wear them and get pleasure out of them.

To show how strong this tradition is, there's even a Jewish charity dedicated to the needs of poor brides that accepts donations of wedding gowns from families of women who've recently died and presents each gown to a poor bride of the right size! This charity has been especially active in Israel where most of the young women who were immigrants from Arab countries arrived empty-handed.

I set to work.

I sold Dee's few valuable jewels to an estate buyer. These included her engagement and wedding rings. It was wrenching to sell them, but there was no reason to keep them since I knew that I'd never give them to anyone else. I realized there <u>might</u> be another woman someday--but that would be a different marriage and would deserve its own rings.

Then I let her friends in Redding and Westport divvy up her costume jewelry; whatever remained, I donated to Goodwill. I also donated her everyday clothes to Goodwill, then let her friends from Manhattan have first dibs on her special clothes: an Elizabethan caftan, a David Hayes dress, a Louis Feraud suit, a Scotch House skirt, a woolen coat from Dublin, a red felt hat from San Francisco, and a straw sun hat from Provence.

The fact that there were only seven of these special items—and originally had been only twelve—was telling. Unlike many women who'd qualify for the Olympics if shopping was a recognized sport, Dee lacked the shopping gene.

But she could be tempted by something beautiful and elegant such as the Elizabethan caftan she came across in the collection of a private designer in Carmel. "Oh, Herb." She swooned. "It's beaded, it's jeweled, it's gorgeous! But when will I ever wear it?"

She needn't have worried. She loved it so much, she found occasions: a gala at the Metropolitan Museum, a formal picnic at Glyndebourne, a Christmas party in La Jolla, a Vladimir Horowitz concert in Paris, and at least half a dozen cruises. "Which proves," she said, "that extravagance is practical, while a sensible purchase that you don't really love is extravagant because you never wear it!"

She decided to give the caftan to a colleague from the Met. "That way, it'll have places to go. It won't just hang in a closet."

Then I asked her about the David Hayes dress she'd worn to Marc's wedding. "Oh God," she giggled, "what a nuisance I was!"

It's true. She had been a nuisance! Because she couldn't find anything "special" in New York, she begged me to drive her to Michigan, where she could be "saved" by her personal shopper at Bonwit's.

"You were very understanding, Herb. You realized that—"

"I realized that a small town like New York had nothing! Absolutely nothing!"

"I know," she said. "It sounds ridiculous, but I was in a panic."

The dress she finally settled on was a bright print in pastel shades. It wasn't a conventional choice for the mother of the groom; it was bolder and more colorful; but she chose it because it was "a happy dress." And now she decided she wanted Cindy to have it. Cindy was a friend from Michigan who always dressed with flair. "A bright print in a David Hayes design—she'll love it!"

I sent the other five pieces to old friends in San Francisco, Los Angeles, Boston, London, and Paris. Dee approved. "Oh good! I'll still be able to travel!"

Finally, her closets were empty, and her clothes were gone; together, we'd set them free.

October 23

Anniversary

Today would've been our forty-sixth anniversary.

Since there was always school in October and we could only get away for a night, we usually celebrated by going to dinner and a show in New York, London, Michigan, or wherever we happened to be living. If the date fell on a Friday or Saturday and we had more time, we'd drive up to the country and spend a weekend at a bed-and-breakfast. On those anniversaries when we both had sabbaticals or flexible schedules, we treated ourselves to vacations at favorite getaways. But our most romantic anniversary by far resulted from a news item.

We'd left Michigan and were living in New York again. One morning, while reading the paper, I came across a surprising item about the Waldorf Astoria hotel. It was offering an anniversary present to couples who'd been married at least forty years, had stayed at the hotel on their wedding night or during a part of their honeymoon, and had the receipt to prove it. The management invited such couples to celebrate their next anniversary at the Waldorf Astoria and pay exactly the same price they'd paid back then.

I showed the item to Dee. She acknowledged that it was a generous offer but didn't think they'd have many takers. "I mean, who keeps a hotel receipt for forty years?"

I bowed and said, "I did."

"You're kidding!"

"Don't you remember? I made a little scrapbook of our honeymoon, beginning with our wedding night at the Waldorf."

"And you know where it is?" she said. "You can actually put your hands on it?"

I crossed to the bookcase, pulled out a small scrapbook, and gave it to her. "Voilà!"

She turned a few pages, smiled, turned a few more, stopped, then gasped. "Do you realize what our room cost in 1955 at the most expensive hotel in New York?"

"Seventy dollars?"

"$16.80!"

But of course, a dollar was different then. In 1955, my father had supported a family of four on an income of six thousand dollars. Dee wondered what the room cost now.

"$435!" I said.

"How do you know?"

"I called out of curiosity."

She was excited. "Oh, Herb, let's do it!"

Right after breakfast, we took a cab to the Waldorf Astoria.

The lobby looked as regal as ever. We met with a hotel rep, showed her our receipt, and made arrangements to spend our next anniversary, which was coming up in two weeks, in the same room we'd had forty-three years ago. Then at her suggestion, we arranged to stay not one night but a weekend.

It was a weekend of happy surprises.

Surprise 1: When we checked in, the room clerk apologetically explained that the room we'd stayed in on our wedding night wasn't available. The current occupant had decided to extend his visit and didn't want to be moved. She hoped we'd understand and would be willing to stay in one of their VIP suites instead. Ever accommodating, we said we'd make do.

Surprise 2: When we entered the suite, there, waiting for us on the table in the sitting room was a magnificent centerpiece of fresh flowers, a bottle of champagne in a bucket of ice, a large bowl of chocolate-covered strawberries, and a card from the Waldorf

Astoria management that said, "Congratulations on your forty-third wedding anniversary! The flowers, champagne, and strawberries are anniversary gifts from the hotel, along with the '55 room rate! Happy weekend!"

Surprise 3: It felt like a second wedding night: five minutes after entering our suite: we were in bed, making love.

Afterward, we relaxed in bed with champagne, strawberries, and memories.

MEMORIES OF MAKING LOVE #1

"Simply Because You're Near Me"

"You know," Dee said, holding out a strawberry for me to bite. "I always thought there was one song that got it exactly right." And she began to sing.

> *I'm in the mood for love*
> *Simply because you're near me.*

I swallowed the strawberry, then joined in.

> *Funny, but when you're near me,*
> *I'm in the mood for love.*

As I poured more champagne, she said, "We never had sex, you know."

I stopped pouring. "We didn't?"

"No, we always made love. Even when it was a quickie, what you called—"

"A target of opportunity."

"Even then, it felt like love."

I finished pouring, then raised my glass in a salute of gratitude. "That's because I never had to cajole or bargain. Sex was never a reward I had to earn. It was always—"

"An exchange of gifts."

I nodded.

"Still," she said, "even though our desires were the same, I realized early on that our appetites were quite different."

"In what way?"

"For me, sex was the dessert at the end of the meal."

"And for me?"

She looked thoughtful, then broke into a mischievous smile. "It could be the dessert, but it could also be the scotch before dinner or the honeydew appetizer or the cucumber soup or the steak and baked potato or even the bread and butter!"

"That's a hell of a meal!"

"Don't I know it!" She became thoughtful again. "But the really incredible thing is that for you, sex wasn't just food. It was medicine. Like the elixir in the Danny Kaye song, it cured everything. If you were tense, it relaxed you. If you were bored, it energized you. If you had a failure, it helped you get over it. If you had a success, it helped you celebrate. And if you felt romantic, it was the gateway to a sweet night."

"Followed by a sweeter morning."

October 24

A Very Serious Argument

I got several calls today from Michigan, from friends who remembered our anniversary and wanted me to know they were thinking of us. I was touched and reminded again of how much we'd enjoyed our fourteen years in Michigan.

Why did we move there? You might say it was because we'd just turned forty. Let me explain.

For a man especially, the forties are a dangerous time. If he doesn't catch the brass ring by then, he feels that his dream of becoming a big success is over and that all he can look forward to is more of the same until retirement. In this mood, he begins to think that the best way to revitalize his life is to fall in love with a young woman who offers the promise of a fresh start.

Dee and I had seen several couples break up for this reason, and we decided to take preemptive measures. The problem, we felt, was that a man needs to be energized by a dream; and if he can't find one in his career, he'll look for it elsewhere. That's why when we turned forty, I decided to leave the safe harbor of television to sail off in the direction of _my_ dream—writing for the theater—and to let our marriage be the anchor of stability in our lives. In my own small way, I felt like Columbus, navigating without a chart across a huge ocean that was reputed to be filled with monsters, and heading for a destination that might not even exist.

And just as Columbus needed Ferdinand and Isabella to finance his venture, I needed a new source of income to finance mine. But what could I do that would pay enough and also give me enough time to write?

During my years in television, as one of the few people around who had a strong academic background—BA, Harvard; MA,

Columbia; fellowship, Yale School of Drama—I was often asked to represent the network at academic conferences. On a number of occasions, after a roundtable or Q and A session, I was approached by a dean or an English department chairman who wanted to know if I'd be interested in switching fields and becoming a professor. I always said no but kept their cards, and now I contacted them. I also spread my net a bit wider and contacted several friends who were professors at other colleges and asked for their help.

After two months, I had four offers. I picked Oakland University in Rochester, Michigan, because it had an excellent English department, a regional theater on campus with a company of professional actors, and was more flexible than the other colleges about granting unpaid leaves to let me write or be involved with productions.

So I left television, where I'd been doing documentaries that won major awards but weren't the plays and musicals I'd dreamed of writing, and became an associate professor of English at Oakland, where I'd finally have time to test myself and find out if I could write for the theater.

It was a huge change from television to academia, from a higher income bracket to a lower one, from the East Coast to the Midwest, and from Manhattan to a suburb of Detroit. But for me, it was a good change. I enjoyed teaching. I began writing my plays and musicals, and soon they began to be produced in regional theaters throughout America and England and in an off-West End theater in London.

For Dee though, the adjustment was harder. Although she found a position as a teacher at the Brookside School of Cranbrook, a prestigious private school whose landmark buildings and grounds had been designed by Eliel Saarinen, Michigan took a lot of getting used to. In fact, early on, it was the cause of one of the most serious arguments we ever had.

Shortly after our move there, I came home on a Friday afternoon to find Dee waiting for me in the front hall with her bags packed.

"Please drive me to the airport," she said. "I'm going back to New York. It's too lonely here."

I was knocked for a loop and sputtered that she couldn't be serious. "We haven't even been here a month."

"Maybe not," she said, "but it's long enough for me to know that I'm too lonely. You don't understand because you don't have the same attachment to friends and places that I do. For you, a friend is someone to <u>do</u> things with—play tennis, go to a ballgame, a movie, a concert. For me, a friend is someone to <u>be</u> with, to share my life with. It takes <u>years</u> to make that kind of friend."

"But," I protested, "<u>I'm</u> here, and <u>Marc's</u> here."

Yes, she admitted, and that meant a lot. But it didn't mean everything. She needed the daily warmth of friends and people she'd known all her life. And that wasn't all. She was a city girl; she liked to <u>walk</u> to stores and to chat with the fruit man, the women in the bakery, the guys in the deli. She was also a New Yorker. She missed dropping in on the spur of the moment at the Met or the Frick or the Modern. She missed concerts at Lincoln Center and the Green Room afterward and late supper with Loren and Dobbie—wonderful friends who helped us become insiders in the world of classical music, where Loren was a world-renowned bassoonist. She missed hopping in a cab at seven o'clock and getting to Broadway in time for a show. She missed walking along Fifth and Madison. She missed a bookstore on every other corner. She missed her neighborhood restaurants—brunch at Barney Greengrass and dinner at Scaletta. Most of all, she missed shopping at Zabar's. She said, "Do you remember during Khrushchev's visit to America, they put a sign in the window: 'God bless America. In Russia, even Khrushchev doesn't eat this good!'"

All these things might be true, I acknowledged, but they weren't exactly a surprise. We'd talked about them before. "You <u>knew</u> you'd miss New York."

"But I didn't know how much." And then she asked me again to please drive her to the airport.

"I can't," I said. "You have to give this a chance. You're looking at Michigan and seeing all the things it isn't. Why not see what it is?" She heard me out patiently. She conceded that for people born in Michigan, it was God's country. But she was also very stubborn and insisted that to her, it was a foreign country. "Fine," I said. "Then why not treat it like a foreign country? Be curious, try new things, have an adventure."

"Because this isn't a visit. It's a permanent relocation!"

"But we signed contracts!"

"Then you stay, and I'll go."

I made a great effort to speak slowly and quietly. "Dee, we have an incredible marriage. We'd be crazy to put it at risk."

"You could fly home on weekends."

But, I pleaded, I didn't want a weekend marriage.

She didn't either, but unfortunately, she felt that she didn't have any choice. She was absolutely convinced she'd die if she stayed in Michigan. I took her hand, pressed it gently, and entered into negotiations. "Promise to stay till June, when our contracts are up. Then, if you're still unhappy, we'll go back to New York." She didn't think she could last that long, but after a few tears and another round of negotiations, she reluctantly agreed.

And then slowly, imperceptibly, hardly knowing it was happening, she began to fall in love with Michigan—with cider and donuts at the local cider mill; with University of Michigan football games and tailgate parties; with restaurants and bakeries in Greektown; with cross-country skiing at Cranbrook; with using Detroit as a jumping-off point for visits to Chicago, Toronto, and Ottawa; and with becoming part of a community that was made up not just of teaching colleagues or writers and artists but people who worked in the automotive industry— strange creatures we'd never seen up close before.

A foreign country indeed. But an interesting one, and eventually, a friendly one, as the calls that morning had reminded me.

November 7

Stronger than Superman

Dee was still getting mail at A Child's Place, so I stopped by once a week to collect it. But I had another reason for stopping by today. Sandy, the new executive director who'd been Dee's assistant and good friend, thought it would be nice to have two of Dee's watercolors on permanent display in the library.

I agreed. That <u>would</u> be nice and appropriate. After all, the library had been Dee's idea; she'd arranged for students at the Harvard Graduate School of Design to work on it as a class project; and at the ceremonial opening, Frances had announced that, by unanimous vote, the board had decided to name the library in Dee's honor.

The two watercolors I'd chosen, had framed, and now carried under my arm were illustrations from *Sometimes . . . Other Times*, a children's book that Dee and I had collaborated on. This simple story, which has not yet been published, is about a young boy who sometimes acts like a little kid and other times like a grown-up, alternating, as children always do, between the safety of dependence and the risk of independence.

In the first illustration, the little kid is being hugged by his mother, and the text reads:

> *Sometimes*
> *when I get tired*
> *I fall down on my rug,*
>
> *Or better yet*
> *I find a place*
> *inside my mommy's hug.*

Sometimes
when I get tired
I fall down on my rug,

Or better yet
I find a place
inside my mommy's hug.

In the second illustration, the little kid feels like a grown-up and climbs to the top of the monkey bars; the text reads:

But other times
I like to climb
the mountainous monkey bars

And when I'm at the top
reach my arms out
to the stars.

But other times
I like to climb
The mountainous monkey bars

And when I'm at the top,
Reach my arms out
To the stars.

When the framed pictures were in place on the wall of the library, several teachers, including Loretta and Sally, came in for a first look. And thereby hangs a tale—for although no one on the staff knew it, Loretta and Sally had inspired one of Dee's unsung triumphs at A Child's Place.

Loretta was a veteran teacher at the school; talented and devoted, she was adored by children and parents alike. But not, at that time, by her young associate teacher, Sally.

One afternoon, at the close of the school day, Sally knocked on Dee's door, came in, and without saying a word, put her resignation on Dee's desk.

Dee was stunned and asked her why? What had happened?

Sally said she couldn't take it anymore. "I'm twenty-eight years old and have five years of classroom experience, but Loretta treats me like a student teacher. She won't let me draw up lesson plans or meet with parents or write student evaluations or do anything but act as class housekeeper. I deserve better. But I won't get it here, not with Loretta, so I'm resigning."

Dee responded sympathetically. "I understand how you feel. What's more, your feelings are justified. But you're a fine young teacher, and Loretta is a legend at A Child's Place. I don't want to lose either of you. Please let me think about this overnight. Let me try to figure out a way to stop this train wreck."

Sally thought it was hopeless and predicted that even Superman couldn't stop this wreck.

Dee advised her to have wine with dinner and, before dropping off to sleep, to keep repeating, "Dee is stronger than Superman. Dee is stronger than Superman."

Over dinner, Dee was in a funk. She had absolutely no idea what to do. She knew she'd bungled. If she'd been on top of things, she would've picked up on Sally's frustration and intervened long ago. But Sally hadn't complained, other matters had been more pressing, and the sore had festered.

That night, Dee stayed up past midnight trying to figure out a solution. The easy one, unfortunately, she had to reject. She couldn't just order Loretta to do what Sally wanted; it would've been too insulting. And even if it hadn't driven Loretta to resign, the relationship between the two women would've been poisoned.

But if she couldn't order Loretta, what <u>could</u> she do? Logically, there was only one alternative: she could persuade her. But how?

The next thing I knew, it was eleven in the morning, and Dee was calling me from her office. "How'd you like to take me to dinner at the Spinning Wheel tonight?"

"What're we celebrating?"

"My solution."

"You squared the circle?"

"I did."

And then at dinner, she revealed her diabolical plot. "I asked Loretta to meet me before school at the Sherwood diner. As soon as we were seated, I told her we had to do something about Sally. 'She's a fine young teacher,' I said, 'but she isn't pulling her weight. She isn't doing as much as she should. The problem is, she lacks confidence.' Before Loretta could object, I plowed on. 'Now you're the only one on the staff who can help her. You know her best, and she thinks you're a god. She'll listen to what you'll say.'

"Loretta was a bit confused. 'What <u>will</u> I say?' I pretended to think, then suggested, 'Something like this. Beginning next week, tell her you expect her to draw up the lesson plans for the class. And on parent-teacher night next month, you expect her to take half the conferences. And at the end of the year, you expect her to write half the student evaluations.' Then I ended by holding my finger up and whispering conspiratorially. 'Now this is crucial. When we get back to my office and tell Sally what we've decided, you'll have to be firm. If she's frightened and says she can't do it, just say, 'Trust me, you can. You have hidden resources.'

"And so it came to pass. And they ended up hugging each other!"

That night, at the Spinning Wheel, I couldn't help noting: "The question before the House is this: Is Dee Appleman a superb executive or a subtle Machiavelli?"

She began to blush, then burst out laughing.

November 8

College of Two

Today I went to view Dee's memorial exhibit at the Mark Twain Library in Redding. It was all that I could've asked for. I stayed in the exhibit area talking to people, including our neighbors, Marjorie and Bill. They said many kind things about the exhibit, then invited me to join them for lunch at the Station House restaurant.

Since it was an Indian summer day, we sat outside on the little front porch. Then Marjorie said, "You know, Dee and I had coffee on this porch last spring. She was in a reflective mood and told me how much she owed you. She said she could never have become a headmistress if you hadn't taught her how to speak in public."

In our conversation that night, Dee said, "It's true, you know. You took a person who'd always been terrified when she had to speak in public and turned her into a person who could face a large audience and speak without notes and without fainting."

"I could only do it," I said, "because you knew your stuff. That's the key. If you know your subject well enough, whatever you say will be right."

Dee objected that I made it sound too easy. "Don't forget, you worked with me every night for three weeks, and you taught me how to use questions." She was referring to the fact that I changed her idea of what a speech is. Almost everyone who's ever given a speech knows that the most enjoyable part of the experience for the speaker is the question-and-answer session after the speech is over. It follows then that the best way to make the whole experience enjoyable is to structure the speech itself as a question-and-answer session.

Dee caught on immediately. "And that way, you guarantee that all your answers are brilliant because you've chosen all the questions!"

"Exactly!"

"Once I understood that," Dee said, "I didn't have to worry about memorizing or pontificating. I could just speak in a conversational tone and be myself." Then she remembered another bit of help I'd provided. "You gave me permission to be nervous. You explained that everyone who speaks in public is nervous, but the experienced speaker learns <u>not</u> to fight it because that just undermines her confidence and concentration. And sure enough, once I let myself <u>be</u> nervous, being nervous gave me a jolt of energy."

"In a few months," I recalled, "you were stepping up to the platform with confidence, speaking in a firm voice, and charming the pants off the audience."

"I don't know about that," Dee said. "But at least I wasn't fainting."

Then it was <u>my</u> turn to say thanks. "I could never have survived as a husband if you hadn't taught me what a woman wants. Freud thought it was impossible to know, but you made it perfectly clear. You said, 'When she feels strong—'"

"She wants to be treated as a mature adult."

"When she feels vulnerable—"

"As someone who needs a shoulder to lean on."

"When she feels sexy—"

"As a hot chick."

"When she <u>doesn't</u> feel sexy—"

"As a friend."

"And always, she expects a man who loves her—"

"To know exactly what mood she's in without being told!"

December 9

Birthday Surprise

Today was my sixty-eighth birthday, and because it was the first one in forty-six years without Dee, it didn't feel like a birthday. So I decided to have a party hosted by memory.

The birthday I chose to remember was my fiftieth, which was celebrated in Williamsburg, Virginia.

We'd left Richmond, where *A Perfect Gentleman*, my comedy about Lord Chesterfield, had received very good reviews and played to sold-out houses at the Virginia Museum Theater.

Witty, Charming, and Beautifully Written
(Jon Longaker, *Richmond Times-Dispatch*).

Refreshingly Civilized, Eloquent, and Loving
(Roy Proctor, *Richmond News Leader*).

We were on our way to Philadelphia, where the same production would open at the Walnut Street Theater. A month before, we'd made arrangements to stop over in Williamsburg for my birthday. But there was an element of mystery involved, for Dee had brought along an extra suitcase.

Saturday night came. Dee had promised to let me open the suitcase at seven o'clock. But at seven o'clock, she changed the timetable. "Let's wait till seven thirty." Then at seven thirty, she said, "Let's go in to dinner and save the suitcase for later."

All through dinner, she kept looking anxiously at her watch.

Then at nine o'clock, I felt a tap on my shoulder and turned around . . . to see Marc!

He'd just flown in from San Diego, where he worked as a sportswriter in the San Diego bureau of the *Los Angeles Times*. As a staff reporter, he covered the Padres, the Chargers, the Sockers, the San Diego State basketball and football teams, and horse racing at Del Mar. He was doing what he'd always wanted to do: living out the fantasy of every literate American who loves sports but isn't good enough to be a professional athlete.

His flight had been delayed two hours, and he'd had to take a commuter flight from Richmond to Newport News, and a car from the airport in Newport News to the tavern in Williamsburg. But here he was, in time to wish me happy birthday.

A bottle of champagne had been cooling in an ice bucket; the wine steward took it out, uncorked it, and filled our glasses.

Marc toasted to my fiftieth birthday, and Dee toasted to our sharing more happy surprises in the years to come.

Then I asked, "What's in the suitcase?"

Dee laughed. "Marc's winter clothes in case there's a cold spell."

December 15

An Adventure with Greg Peck

A Perfect Gentleman also pleased critics and audiences in Philadelphia.

'Gentleman' Triumphant!
(Nels Nelson, *Philadelphia Daily News*).

Stylish, Touching Play Is Just About Perfect
(Robert Baxter, *Courier-Post*).

And this is how Philip F. Crosland ended his review in the Wilmington News Journal:

A Perfect Gentleman restores one's faith in the ability of a contemporary playwright to deal majestically with the English language.

A few days after the opening, we returned to Michigan.

About a week later, I was working at my desk when the phone rang. I picked it up and heard a voice that I couldn't place but that was definitely familiar.

"Is Mr. Appleman there?"

"Yes. This is Herb Appleman."

"Good. I'm glad I caught you in. This is Gregory Peck."

Now I knew why the voice was familiar.

"I've just read *A Perfect Gentleman*. My agent saw the reviews from Richmond and Philadelphia, was very impressed, got her hands on a script, and sent it to me with Broadway in mind."

Aha, I thought, there is a God, after all.

"I'm calling," Peck continued, "because I wanted to tell you personally that I think it's a wonderful play but—"

"Does there have to be a <u>but</u>?"

"I'm afraid so. As much as I like the play—and the part—I don't think critics or audiences will accept me as an eighteenth-century English lord. I've been pegged as an American and every time I play someone who <u>isn't</u> American, I get clobbered. I can write the review in advance: 'Mr. Peck tries his best, but his best isn't good enough. He's simply not convincing as an English lord.'"

I couldn't let this chance be destroyed by an imaginary review. "You may be right," I said, "but I'll risk it if you will."

"I won't," he said. Then he quickly added, "But I didn't call just to disappoint you. I may be able to help after all."

I waited, confused but hopeful. "How, Mr. Peck?"

"Please call me Greg."

"Okay, Greg. <u>How</u> can you help?"

"Well, the thing is--may I call you Herb?"

"Sure. Absolutely!"

"Well, Herb, the thing is, I want to <u>produce</u> *A Perfect Gentleman*." Before I had a chance to get over my surprise, he went on. "I know you're wondering, What the hell does Greg Peck know about producing? Well, I don't want to blow my own horn, but for many summers I produced plays at the La Jolla Playhouse. I have hands-on experience. I have access to investors, and I have access to major stars."

I was thrilled by his offer. "That'll be terrific!"

"I was hoping you'd say that. I'll have my lawyer draw up a standard option agreement and send it to you in the next few days."

All I could do was repeat "That'll be terrific!"

"Meanwhile, I have a suggestion about casting." I could tell by the new energy in his voice that he was excited. "Rex Harrison is an old pal of mine. He's also my next-door neighbor on the Riviera, so it's easy for me to get to him. What do you think of Rex as Lord Chesterfield?"

"I think he'd be terrific!" (Oh my god, wasn't there any other word I knew?)

"All right then. I'll hand the script to Rex personally. And as soon as he gives me an answer, I'll call you." Then he issued a warning. "But don't sit by the phone waiting. He's a great procrastinator. It'll take some time."

"I'll be patience itself." Then I signed off. "Well, Greg, thanks for the call. It's been good talking to you."

"Actually," he said, "I think it's been terrific."

Rex was indeed a great procrastinator. During the next six months, he read the script a dozen times, refused to make a decision, made a decision, unmade it, and drove me bonkers!

I hadn't heard from Greg in several weeks. Then, in June, when Dee and I were back in our Manhattan apartment for the summer, he called.

It was a Friday morning, and I'd just gone down to get the mail. Dee answered the phone.

"Hello," the voice said, "this is Greg Peck. Is Herb there?"

"No," Dee said as calmly as she could. "He's downstairs, getting the mail. But I expect him back in a few minutes."

"Would you ask him to call me when he gets back?"

"Do I have to?"

"I beg your pardon."

"I'd much rather keep talking to you for the next few minutes."

"About what?"

"It doesn't matter. Anything."

"Why?"

"So that afterward you can tell all your friends you just talked to Dee Appleman."

"Oh, I see," he chuckled. "Well then, what'll we talk about?"

Dee didn't have to think long. "Why don't we talk about *Roman Holiday*?"

"My pleasure. I have nothing but happy memories of that picture. From the first take, it was clear that Audrey was a natural. And since Willie Wyler, our director, was at the top of his game, the joy on the set showed up on the screen. It's a movie—"

"That has everything, including a very funny Greg Peck."

"Thank you."

"For me, your best scene is the one at the Mouth of Truth when you pull your arm out, and it looks as if the Mouth has bitten your hand off."

"I stole that gag from Red Skelton."

"The first time I saw it, I reacted just as Audrey did. I jumped out of my skin!"

"You were supposed to!"

Then I returned, and Dee held out the phone to me, saying nonchalantly, "It's Greg."

I took the phone and tried to be equally nonchalant, but couldn't pull it off. "Tell me," I blurted nervously, "what's the final verdict?"

Greg was cautious. "It's hard to say."

"What do you mean?"

It seems that Rex was inclined to do *A Perfect Gentleman*-- but only if his son, Noel, would play Philip. "It's brilliant casting-- a famous father and his little-known son played by a famous father and his little-known son. There's only one problem—Noel turned us down."

"In God's name, why?"

"That's what I want you to find out. As it happens, Noel is appearing in *Blithe Spirit* this week, at the Ivoryton Playhouse in Connecticut, about a two-hour drive from Manhattan. As a courtesy to me, he's willing to meet with you tomorrow after the matinee. I know it's a long drive, back and forth, but I think it's worth a try. After all, it's very flattering to have the playwright come, hat in hand, to plead with you, and Noel hasn't been flattered often in his life."

The next day, I drove up to the Ivoryton Playhouse.

Noel Harrison couldn't have been nicer. He praised *A Perfect Gentleman,* then explained, with painful honesty, why I was asking the impossible. "You don't know my father. He's enormously talented, but he's not a kind man. If I played opposite him, he'd act me off the stage at every performance. Eight times a week, he'd wipe up the floor with me. In two months, three at the outside, I'd have a breakdown. That's why I have to say no. After a lifetime as Rex's son, I've learned to protect myself. You see, it's either your play or my sanity."

All too soon, Greg ran out of casting ideas and dropped his option. To soften the blow, he delivered the news over lunch at the Four Seasons. "I'm sorry," he said, "but as you've learned by now, most productions <u>don't</u> happen. Hell, I've been trying to get someone to do a remake of *Dodsworth* for eight years!" He gave a deep sigh and looked at me apologetically. "I hope you can forgive me for failing you."

I wanted to say "I can't. You gave up too quickly."

But Dee sensed my resentment and, knowing that it would serve no good purpose, intervened. "I look at it this way," she said. "It's another near miss, another almost, another disappointment. But on the bright side, it'll make a good story for Herb's memoir."

Greg reached across the table, took Dee's hand, and gallantly kissed it. Then he turned to me and whispered, but loud enough for Dee to hear, "She's a keeper."

December 18

Snowflakes

With the holiday season approaching, I sent out Dee's *Snowflakes* card.

She'd painted four watercolors for a set of greeting cards of the four seasons.

The winter card was a close-up of snowflakes. The flakes were like crystals of light blue set against a background of darker blue, creating an impression of winter as beauty.

Because snowflakes are nondenominational, it made a perfect holiday card.

We used to write "Happy Chanukah" to our Jewish relatives and friends;

"Merry Christmas" to our Christian friends;

"Season's Greetings" to our atheist, agnostic, and secular humanist friends;

And "Joy of Winter" to our many friends of the skiing persuasion.

Snowflakes

December 20

Nude Lovers Floating on Air

A Christmas memory.

On Christmas break, during Dee's freshman year, I took her gallery hopping on Madison Avenue. I thought it would be just a looking expedition, but I wound up buying her a print of Marc Chagall's painting, *Adam and Eve in Paradise*, which we immediately renamed *Nude Lovers Floating on Air*.

The print cost thirty-five dollars, which should've put it out of my price range—that was a lot of money in 1951, especially for a college student—but Dee loved it so much I decided to splurge.

Over the years, that print has hung in every apartment and every house we've lived in.

A coda to this story: Marc Chagall became a permanent part of our lives in another and even more significant way—we named our son after him. And when Chagall came to New York to do the sets and costumes for *The Magic Flute*, we arranged for our Marc, who was then seven, to meet him.

Dee took along a photo portrait of Chagall that a friend had given us when Marc was born, and Chagall graciously signed it, *Pour Marc de Marc*.

December 31

A Very Special New Year's Eve

Holidays are notoriously hard when you're alone.

Tonight was New Year's Eve. Jack and Laura—good friends with whom we often shared evenings in the theater and other special occasions—invited me to join them for the bash at the Harvard Club, but I didn't feel up for a gala evening in Manhattan.

Still, I didn't want to be alone, so I drove up the road to Clemens, my favorite restaurant in Redding. The owners, Eva and John, took special pains with my holiday dinner, sat down to drink a glass of champagne with me, and did whatever they could to make the evening festive. I stayed to toast the New Year, then left shortly after midnight.

Alone in a quiet house, I found myself thinking of other years when Dee and I had just come home from a New Year's Eve party.

MEMORIES OF MAKING LOVE #2

WOW!

Inevitably, I thought of 1955, when we were grad students at Yale and had only been married nine weeks. After a terrific party with other grad students, we returned to our apartment around 2:00 a.m.

We'd already reached that point in our love and lovemaking where we could share uncensored desires and fantasies.

Lying in bed, lit by an erotic glow that had gotten rosier as the party had gotten merrier, we confided this and that and playfully tried that and this--until somehow, we stumbled on WOW!

O the paradoxical wonder of Dee! She was refined, gracious, and a perfect lady. She never dressed provocatively or acted seductively.

But in the playground of our marriage bed, she was sensual and adventurous. As a husband, I knew I had struck gold. Dee was the wife and friend I had prayed for and the lover I was sure only existed in my fantasies but who now made those fantasies real every night.

And never more so than on New Year's Eve in 1955, when we discovered WOW!

Today, people can look it up on the internet, talk about it on radio call-in shows, and read articles about it in any women's magazine.

But in 1955, we hadn't even <u>heard</u> of WOW!

During the next few months, we often considered writing an anonymous letter to *Playboy* to let others in on the big secret--but we never did, because we didn't think most people, even readers of *Playboy*, were ready for WOW!

It sounds ridiculous, but we really thought we were the first couple in history who'd ever done this. Then one day, Dee came home with a sheepish smile. She'd been to the beauty parlor, where she'd overheard two women talking about WOW!

Only they called it oral sex.

To hear them tell it, WOW! had been around since ancient Greece and Rome.

It was deflating to find out that we'd reinvented the wheel, but we were still proud of our daring and of the love and trust that had made it possible.

January 1

A Bench in Berkeley Square

After reliving the discovery of WOW! I fell into a deep sleep; and obeying the wayward logic of dreams, I was soon dreaming of the last time Dee and I had spent New Year's Day in London.

The day began with breakfast at Richoux, followed by a stroll through the neighborhood of Mayfair. Though Mayfair was usually crowded with shoppers and guests from the elegant hotels on Park Lane, it was as quiet as a suburb on New Year's morning.

At a corner grocery, run by an Indian family we'd befriended, we bought the morning papers, then continued our stroll until we reached Berkeley Square. This was one of our favorite haunts in London: a garden oasis in the middle of town and a romantic oasis where many of the benches had plaques with personal inscriptions.

We found an empty bench, spread out our papers—the *London Times*, the *Herald Tribune*, the tabloids with the most sensational headlines—and treated ourselves to a heady mixture of scandals and serious matters. It was a mild winter day, and we enjoyed sitting out in the open air. For over an hour, we read and talked and fed the birds; then slowly we headed out of the Square, pausing every few yards to study an inscription and imagine the story behind it.

Suddenly, the purpose of my dream became clear—I was going to buy a plaque for a bench in the Square, and the inscription on the plaque would read:

For my lovely Dee and our mornings in London--
breakfast, a walk, a bench in this garden.
Ever & always, Herb

February 1

Two Truths

Throughout our lives, Dee and I loved to write each other letters. During the years I was at Harvard and Dee was at Syracuse, we wrote several letters a week. Later, when I was out of town with a play or musical that was in rehearsal, we wrote almost every day. Usually, the subjects of these letters were "I miss you" or "I want to share this with you," but on rare occasions, the subject was "This is something painful that has to be said."

Today, I came across such a letter that had been tucked away in the back of an old file cabinet. I felt it should be included in this memoir because disappointment and heartache are part of every story.

Dear Herb,

This year, we were sentenced to Hell.

My mother had Parkinson's, my father had Alzheimer's, your mother had an emergency tracheotomy, and your father had a heart attack and died.

We spent our weekends and free time after work going from one hospital to another. It was exhausting and depressing. Lin shared the burden of caring for your mother. But no one could help us with my parents—I was the only family they had in New York.

Finally, after seven months, you told me we had to stop.

"There's no point to it," you said. "Your mother doesn't recognize you and your father doesn't recognize <u>anyone</u>."

I told you I <u>had</u> to visit them. "If I stop, it'll seem as if they're already dead."

You were very sympathetic but said we'd done all we could, and now had to think of ourselves and our <u>own</u> family.

I accused you of letting me down.

You said I was asking too much of us.

We continued living at arm's length until my parents died.

The experience left us with scars but taught us two truths: the strongest love can be damaged if the sky falls in, and love that's been damaged can be repaired--if the love is strong enough.

As ever,
Dee

February 14

Valentine's Day

The cancer was taking its toll, and Dee had been feeling low all day.

I wanted to cheer her up. But how?

While she napped in the afternoon, I drove to Ridgefield, went into a dozen shops, and looked at scarves, earrings, elegant art books, and a cornucopia of holiday gifts; but nothing spoke to me.

Discouraged, I started back for Redding.

And then I had a brain wave, turned the car around, drove to the Ridgefield library, and spent the next two hours in a study room, writing.

When Dee sat down to dinner, there was an envelope on her place mat. Inside the envelope, she found this lyric.

Sometimes

Man is by nature polygamous.
Passion, we know, doesn't last.
Love is mere sentimentality
From the Victorian past.
But sometimes against all the odds
A couple is blessed by the gods.

Sometimes,
Not often, but sometimes,
Love leads to passion, and then
Passion leads back to love
And the cycle starts over again.

Sometimes,
Not often, but sometimes,
Love comes and magically stays.
This time
Is one of those sometimes,
A time that will last
For the rest of our days.

MEMORIES OF MAKING LOVE #3

Something Very Nice Began To Happen.

That night in bed, despite being very tired, Dee somehow found the energy, the desire, and the will to turn love into passion. We cuddled close in the spoon position, and she pressed against me, and I pressed back, and something very nice began to happen.

Fifty years ago, love had come… and magically it had stayed.

One delightful bit of evidence is that we'd never stopped wanting each other. It was a quiet kind of wanting: like the heating rack in the bathroom of our London flat, it didn't make noise and it didn't light up, but it was always on. And that's why when we got into bed and snuggled close, nice things happened.

March 5

High and Low in Paris

Today I got an email from Jacques and Denise in Paris, wondering how I was faring and inviting me to visit them. "A change of scene will do you good," they said.

Jacques and Denise had once sublet our Manhattan apartment for a year. On our trips to New York during that year—over Thanksgiving, Christmas, and spring break—we went out with them several times: to a revival of *Porgy and Bess*, to hear Barbara Cook at the Carlyle, and to see a Yankees game. They were a charming couple, and we became friends.

It was kind of them to invite me, and I emailed back, thanking them but declining their invitation. I had no desire to go to Paris. Say *Paris* and the first word I think of is *debacle*.

In 1985, about a year after Peck dropped his option, *A Perfect Gentleman* was optioned by a Parisian producer. One day, he sent me the following telegram: "Am completing negotiations with Jean-Pierre Aumont to head cast, Hubert de Givenchy to design costumes, and the Louvre to provide, on loan, authentic period furniture. Will hold press conference in ten days. Please come."

Ten days was just enough time for me to arrange a crossing on the *QE2*, paid for by three lectures on the American musical—a very affordable price.

On board the *QE2*

After docking at Southampton, we took a car to Heathrow and, from Heathrow, flew to Orly. Arriving in Paris, we were buoyant.

Backstory:

A Perfect Gentleman is a comedy set in London in 1755 about the conflict between Lord Chesterfield, an English statesman and wit who has great political ambitions for his illegitimate son, Philip, and Philip, who has other ambitions for himself.

On the occasion of its first production in England, reporters were curious about the presumptuous American who dared to write a comedy of manners about an English lord.

The following interview appeared in the theatre programme:

Q: How did you, an American, happen to write a play about Lord Chesterfield?

A: I first came across Lord Chesterfield as an undergraduate at Harvard. I was taking a survey course in English lit, and we were assigned Chesterfield's *Letters to His Son*. I read them and was really ticked off. *My God,* I thought, *what a selfish old bastard to put such pressure on his son.*

Then, years later, after I'd married and had a son of my own, I took another look at Chesterfield's letters.

Lo and behold, I now found myself sympathizing with Lord Chesterfield! He was obviously a good man who loved his son very much and took great pains on his behalf.

It immediately struck me that since I could now identify equally with father and son, this was a perfect subject for me to write about, because what interests me most as a playwright is the conflict between Right and Right.

Q: But if you wanted to do a father-son play, why didn't you update the story? Why did you stick to the eighteenth-century background?

A: I was tired of the conventional modern play in which dialogue is usually reduced to grunts and curses, costumes range from blue jeans to no jeans, and the set is as dingy as possible.

I wanted to write dialogue that was witty, for characters who could be dressed elegantly and presented in a setting that was unashamedly beautiful.

It's probably true that, before the Angry Young Men, the theater had prettified life too much. But in recent years, I think the pendulum has swung too far in the other direction. I wanted to restore a balance, to remind the audience of certain civilized values that were now being neglected: not only the pleasures of good talk, lovely women, and beautiful things, but the virtue of compromise, the inevitability of imperfection, and the possibility of conflict that doesn't destroy affection and end in estrangement.

Q: How much of the play is quotation, and how much has been invented by you?

A: For better or worse, 99 percent of *A Perfect Gentleman* is mine.

A PERFECT GENTLEMAN

A Page from the Final Scene

PHILIP: According to his lordship, every man, no matter how brilliant or how selfish, has at least one passion that he can't master. The Duke of Newcastle accepts bribes.

JEANNIE: And his lordship?

PHILIP: I hesitate to say, it will seem immodest—

JEANNIE: Now, Phil, don't play games with us—speak up—

LORD C: Yes, what is his lordship's ruling passion?

PHILIP: Why, sir, it's his love for me—

JEANNIE: But I thought his love for you was very practical: obey me and I love you, don't and I don't.

PHILIP: No doubt it seemed so. But consider: despite all my bumbling, all the ways I disappointed him, he continued to believe that I was capable of greatness. Was that practical? Then consider all the gifts that he lavished on me: Time . . . Thought . . . Endless Care. By comparison, it's nothing to give a boy money. But to pay with yourself, to hope and scheme for a child, to risk humiliation for him, and then to beg his forgiveness because—indeed there is no because—these, I submit, are proofs of love. And if still more proof is needed, I have a thousand letters that will bear witness to it.

LORD C: Ah, dear boy . . .

> (Quickly covers his emotion with a touch of wit)
> If only you'd spoken like that in Parliament . . . No
> matter. We've met each other half way. And now,
> if you like, for the sake of appearances, you may
> embrace me.

Poster Credit: Birmingham Repertory Theatre, UK

Over the years, the play has been produced with success on both sides of the Atlantic. In America, it won the American Playwrights Theater Award.

That's the good news. The bad news is that *A Perfect Gentleman* has been optioned twice for Broadway, four times for the West End, and once for Paris—and has yet to be produced in any of these venues. The irony is that Paris began on such a high note.

On the recommendation of Garson Kanin, we made reservations at the Hotel Raphael. Not that we knew Garson Kanin, but in his biography, *Tracy and Hepburn*, he mentioned that the Raphael was the hotel they stayed at whenever they came to Paris: it had Gallic charm, original Turners in the lobby, and an interesting mix of guests from classical music, theater and film, art, publishing, and finance.

The Raphael lived up to its billing. We hadn't been in the hotel ten minutes when we stepped into the elevator and were joined a moment later by Vladimir Horowitz and his manager.

I recognized Horowitz at once, by his face and by his extremely nervous behavior. He wiped his forehead with his handkerchief, put the handkerchief back very carefully in his breast pocket, took the handkerchief out again, wiped his forehead again, and put the handkerchief back very carefully in his breast pocket.

Tonight would be his first concert in Paris in many years, and it was well known that he always suffered from nervous anxiety on the day of a concert. So I took it upon myself to buck him up. "Mr. Horowitz," I said, "I can't help noticing that you seem nervous. I want to assure you, you have no reason to be. My wife and I were at your concert in New York last month, and in our opinion, you weren't half bad."

He stared at me in disbelief, then threw his head back and laughed loudly. "Did you hear that?" he asked his manager. "In their opinion, I wasn't half bad."

"As a matter of fact," I added, "you were pretty good."

"Did you hear that?" he repeated. "As a matter of fact, I was pretty good!"

Seeing that Mr. Horowitz was enjoying himself, I continued in the same vein. "I have every confidence that you'll get through tonight's concert without any trouble."

"Not even a little trouble?" he asked. By this time, his body had relaxed, and he was giggling.

"No," I said, "I'm sure you'll play as you always do—magnificently."

Then his manager said, "I congratulate you. It's not easy to make Mr. Horowitz laugh on the day of a concert. Would you like tickets for this evening?"

I said we'd love tickets for that evening. Dee said she'd wear her Elizabethan caftan. We were elated and felt our serendipitous meeting with Horowitz was a good omen. Paris was going to be lucky for us.

And it was, until the next morning, when our producer dropped by unexpectedly.

"I regret it is a debacle!" he said mournfully. "We have done the budget. The production I have planned is too expensive, and we cannot cut corners. This production must be done in the grand style or not at all. I am sorry. Reality is our enemy, and it is too strong for us." Then like the devil disappearing in a puff of smoke, he was gone.

A Turning Point

Suddenly, the fight went out of me. There are just so many times you can go into battle. I was tired of being shot at and tired of being wounded. I wanted to declare an armistice and retreat to the university.

But Dee wouldn't let me. "Just because a decision doesn't turn out the way you hoped it would, that doesn't mean it's wrong. It just means life is a bitch. Anyhow, you've <u>been</u> a professor. That part of your life is over. <u>This</u> part is for writing."

She was trying to comfort me, but I was afraid she was offering false comfort. "What'll we use for money?" I asked.

She didn't see that as a problem. "We can get by on my salary."

"For how long?"

"As long as we have to, which I'm sure won't be as long as you think. The productions will come."

I quoted Ben Franklin. "He who lives on hope dies fasting."

Dee dismissed the quote with an airy wave. "No," she said, "he who lives on hope, lives." Then, without giving me a chance to object, she went on. "Now tell me, if *A Perfect Gentleman* had been produced in Paris and had been the success it deserved to be, what did you want to write next?"

She was indefatigable, but I was depressed and angry. "You don't understand! I'm not up to it. I don't have the heart to sit at my desk for a year or two, then knock on doors for a year or two, then have the play optioned, then have the option dropped—"

"It doesn't always get dropped."

"Or have the production scheduled then cancelled—"

"It doesn't always get cancelled."

"Or have the play produced and get terrific reviews, maybe even awards, then be done by a handful of regional theaters but still not transfer to Broadway or the West End, and still not change our lives."

Dee's voice softened. She could feel my pain but didn't want to indulge it. "Our lives are changed by the fact that the play exists and is good. Anything else is gravy." And then, after letting that sink in, she said, "Now tell me, what's the new play about?"

I shook my head in resignation and told her. "It's called *Sailing with Magellan*. And it's about my senior year in high school, when my parents wanted me to apply to Brooklyn College and continue to live at home and be on call if my mother had to be hospitalized. But Dr. Orgel, the dean at Lincoln, persuaded me to apply to Harvard. And I <u>did</u>—without telling my parents—and I was <u>accepted</u> on a full scholarship, and then all hell broke loose."

Obviously, I explained, I couldn't write this play while my parents were alive; they would've felt betrayed. "But now they're gone, and I think I have enough perspective and enough love to do them justice. And," I continued, "the theme of the play has more than personal significance. What I learned that year is what we all have to learn eventually—if you turn your back on yourself, your life is without passion or integrity. If you turn your back on those closest to you, your life is without love. And you don't get to choose. You have to strike a balance, but it isn't easy. And no one gets the balance exactly right. You just do the best you can."

Dee had been a writer's wife long enough to know that what was needed at this point was all-out encouragement. "I can't wait," she said, "to hear you read it to me!"

Sailing with Magellan now exists. It hasn't had a major production yet, but I think it's good. Dee thought it was damn good, and anything else is gravy.

*   *   *

Many years later, Marc told me about a conversation he'd had with Dee shortly after our return from that disappointing trip to Paris.

"One afternoon," he said, "I came home and found Mom sitting by the window, crying. I asked her what was wrong, but she just shrugged. "No," I insisted, "tell me."

"Sometimes," she said, wiping her eyes, "it gets to be too hard."

"What does?"

"Living in the Land of Almost." Then she explained. "The best place to live is the Land of Success—that's obvious. And the next best is Failure--because once you get over the pain, Failure is a wake-up call that forces you to try something else. But the worst place—the place that breaks your heart—is Almost."

I was confused. "Doesn't *Almost* mean you're getting close?"

"No. It means you're not close enough. Don't you see, if enough little productions get done and enough little awards get won and enough little bones get thrown your way, you think the grapes are finally within reach."

From the glazed look in my eyes, she realized she'd lost me. "Remember the myth of Tantalus? He was very hungry, and a bunch of grapes was just an inch away. So he reached for them and almost got them but just missed. Then he tried again—God, how he tried!—but trying isn't getting. Still, he refused to give up. He was so hungry, and the grapes were so close--he kept on trying--year after year."

"I don't understand. If you feel that way, why did you encourage Dad to write another play? Why didn't you get him to try something else?

Her eyes became teary again. "Because he's very talented, and he'd only be half alive if he had to do something else. Besides," she added with a sad smile, "there's always the chance that one day he'll finally get to eat those damn grapes!"

April 2

Aristotle Contemplating the Bust of Homer

It seems I'll be traveling after all. Not to Paris but to London.

To view the plaque that's been installed on Dee's bench in Berkeley Square.

Thinking it would be a mistake to cross on the *QE2*—the burden of memory would be too heavy—I asked Cunard to book me on the *Caronia*, a ship that Dee and I had never sailed on, taking a route we'd never traveled. (Unlike the *QE2*, which crossed directly from New York to Southampton in six days, the *Caronia* left from Fort Lauderdale and made a leisurely crossing in two weeks, with stops at Bermuda and the Azores).

When I picked up my ticket at the Cunard office on Fifth Avenue, I couldn't help smiling at the person I'd become. It was hard to believe that Dee and I had grown up thinking the ideal life was solely a matter of the spirit and had nothing to do with pleasures that cost money.

But that ideal was undermined when we saw Rembrandt's painting *Aristotle Contemplating the Bust of Homer*.

We went the first day the Met put the painting on exhibit--and were stunned! Everyone knew Rembrandt was a great painter and Aristotle was a great philosopher. Yet, in this painting, Rembrandt portrayed Aristotle not as a poor man walking barefoot in Athens, like Socrates, but as a man of means, wearing elegant clothes and jewelry.

"If I remember rightly," Dee said, closing her eyes and trying to visualize the painting, "Aristotle's left hand rests on a magnificent golden chain that hangs across his chest. And his right hand rests on the head of an antique bust of Homer. The overall impression is that of a wise man who hasn't cut himself off from the pleasures of the world but has learned to enjoy them as part of a full and balanced life."

It was an eye-opener for us and eventually led to cruises on the *QE2* and house exchanges in La Jolla, Carmel, Basel, and Rome. It even led us, in flush times, to buy a few golden chains.

April 5

On Board the Caronia

At 9:00 a.m., I flew down to Fort Lauderdale; and at 2:00 p.m., I went on board.

It was good to be at sea again: to take a long walk around the lower deck, then stand on the upper deck at midnight and gaze in awe at the brightness of the stars and the immensity of the sky.

But any experience deeply felt wants to be shared, so I imagined Dee standing next to me. We stood for a long time, as we had on other voyages, enjoying the beauty of a quiet night at sea and just being together. Then we found two deck chairs, settled in, and began to chat about ship life.

"How are the people at your table?"

"Nice," I said, "it's a group of five lecturers."

"Anyone like Frank and Ellen in the group?"

"Afraid not."

Dee was referring to Frank and Ellen McCourt. On our last crossing on the *QE2*, we became friends with the McCourts. Frank was a former high school teacher who, shortly after retirement, wrote his first book—a memoir about his harrowing childhood in Ireland. He called the book *Angela's Ashes*, and amazingly, this dark book by an unknown writer became a huge best seller and a Pulitzer Prize winner. As a famous author, he was the featured lecturer on this crossing. He turned out to be an Irish charmer, and his talk to an overflow audience in the Queen's Room was both honest and hilarious.

"The *QE2*," he began, "is a dream world. Everywhere you look, there's glamour and elegance. So what are you people doing here? Why would you come to hear a talk about poverty and ignorance and superstition? Why would you throw such a shadow over your holiday?" And then with a sly smile, he said, "Unless, of course, as you're listening to me, you're saying to yourself, 'Oh, that poor little Frankie McCourt. That poor bastard. Thank God I'm not him!'" As soon as the talk was over, Dee and I introduced ourselves to Frank and Ellen; after a few beers, we felt like old friends.

At sunset, on the last night of the crossing, as the *Caronia* sailed from the Azores to Southampton, I sat in a cocktail bar, lingered over a shandy, listened to an English pianist play Noël Coward songs, and thought, *How strange. Dee and I had lived in New York, Michigan, and Connecticut. We'd traveled all over the world. Yet the scrapbooks of our marriage had more photos, souvenirs, and clippings from England than from anywhere else.*

April 12

41 Ennismore Gardens

The *Caronia* docked early.

Luckily, the flat in South Kensington was available; I unpacked and was settled in by noon.

Fate gave us that flat—fate and Alistair Sim. It happened during the summer of the Silver Jubilee. London was filled with royal well-wishers from every corner of the British Isles and with visiting Canadians, Australians, South Africans, and former colonials from every corner of the British Commonwealth. There wasn't an empty hotel room or flat-to-let in the entire city. But I had to be in London for three months, and since it was summertime, Dee and Marc were able to join me. We were willing to turn our visit into an adventure, but we weren't willing to sleep on the streets for three months.

My agent came to the rescue and arranged for us to sublet the London flat in Hammersmith of Alastair Sim, the droll star of *The Belles of St. Trinian's*, who was out of the country, shooting a movie on location.

When I wrote to Sim that we'd need an extra room for our son, he wrote back, "Not to worry, there is an extra room, and I'm sure it will suit you very nicely."

He was half right. There was an extra room, but it was the size of a shoebox; and instead of a bed, it had a crib. For some reason, Sim had assumed that Marc was a toddler. If so, he was the only toddler in London who was six feet tall and would be spending part of the summer taking courses at Oxford.

We left the key and a note of explanation with the custodian, then stood on the street, feeling lost.

Dee was on the verge of tears, so I hailed a taxi and told the driver to take us to the Dorchester Hotel on Park Lane. I was always a great believer in the Spanish proverb "Living well is the best revenge." I thought lunch at the Dorchester was just what we needed.

Dee complained that it was far too expensive. . . then thanked me.

After lunch, we walked through Mayfair, looking for a to-let sign, preferably one that read, "Spacious flat—tastefully furnished with gorgeous views and affordable rent." For over an hour, we walked up one street and down another, trusting that fate would be our real estate agent; then as we turned into Curzon Street, we saw a moving van outside an apartment building. A young mother was standing near the van, rocking a baby carriage. Dee trotted over to her and asked if she knew the people who were moving in.

The woman said she did.

Then Dee asked, "Do you know if their old flat is still available?"

The woman nodded and said it was. "As it happens, I live in the same building—41 Ennismore Gardens in South Kensington—and the reason I know the flat is still available is because the owners who live in Wiltshire never advertise. They depend on other people in the building to recommend friends or relatives. This way, they feel they have a better chance of getting tenants who are suitable."

"Very wise," Dee said. "And this flat, this available flat with ideal neighbors, is it big enough for the three of us?"

"It should be. Why?"

"Because the flat we subleased sight unseen isn't, and we're desperate. We need a place for three months. This sounds perfect."

"Unless," I quickly threw in, "it's horribly expensive."

"It isn't, is it?" Dee asked, a plea in her voice.

The woman hesitated then said, "I don't think so. Not if you're going to take it for three months."

"Good," Dee said. "Then I have only one more question: Would you be willing to recommend us?"

The woman kept a straight face. "Are you suitable?"

"Actually," Dee confided, "we're three angels."

Of course at that moment, we had no idea that our neighbors would include Ava Gardner, famous to older moviegoers as one of the great beauties of the century, and Charles Gray, famous to younger moviegoers as one of the James Bond villains.

To say that we saw a lot of Ava would be true but misleading. The fact is, she had a flat in an elegant building across the street from us, and our windows and her windows were on the same level; so although we weren't close, we did see a lot of each other. You might say it was a waving relationship.

We also saw Ava quite often at Charles Gray's place. Charles kept an open house for his theatrical chums. In pleasant weather, he'd sit out on his terrace; and if any chums passed by at the cocktail hour, he'd invite them up for a "drinkie." We saw more of them in 1987 after they became fans of *Heyday*, my musical comedy that was produced at the King's Head Theatre in London.

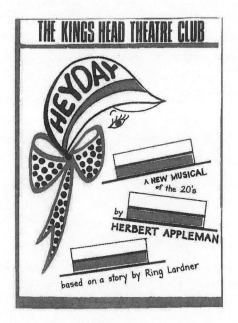

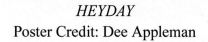

HEYDAY
Poster Credit: Dee Appleman

*"The lightest, fluffiest soufflé of a
'20s musical: **Critics' Choice**"*

--Time Out: London

*"To laugh in the theatre is rare.
(I confess I fell out of my chair!)
And to hear a few hummable tunes
Is like finding a brace of blue moons!"*

--City Limits: London

They were delightful company, except when the empty bottles began to pile up. While we'd nurse a drink, they'd finish a bottle. But there was one night when they got very annoyed with us. "You're too damn sober!" they hissed, and insisted that we prove our friendship by matching them drink for drink.

When we finally left them, we were beyond drunk; as they used to say in the speakeasies, Dee was *pie-eyed* and I was *blotto.*

Ever the gracious host, Charles poured us out of the building. After we tripped over the front step, we looked one way, then the other, gave the matter careful thought, then turned in the wrong direction, and walked all the way to Hyde Park; there we turned ourselves around and walked back in the right direction—but past our house. By a process of elimination, we finally got to number 41 and watched in amazement as the key fit in the lock and the door opened.

Then we had to crawl up the five flights almost completely in the dark. When we finally stumbled into our flat, we collapsed on the bed and slept till the next afternoon.

April 13

"Breakfast, a Walk, a Bench in this Garden"

Around three, we woke up, rubbed the sleep out of our eyes, and—still in our evening clothes—went to the window and pulled up the blinds. Ava happened to be looking in our direction at that moment, saw us, waved, and laughed like crazy!

The neighborhood was glamorous in other ways too. We did our daily shopping in the food stalls at Harrods, our window shopping in the boutiques on Beauchamp Place, and dropped in frequently at the Victoria and Albert Museum, which was only two blocks away.

Now after lunch at the Ennismore Arms pub, I walked through Hyde Park and the streets of Mayfair to Berkeley Square. As I entered the Square, I stepped aside for a young woman who was brown bagging it.

"Going to have your lunch in the Square?" I asked.

"Uh-huh," she said, "my girlfriend and I often do when the weather's nice. And you?"

"I'm going to visit a bench."

She looked at me with new interest. "What's your name? I mean, your first name?"

"Herb."

"No!" she squealed in delight. "Not the Herb of Herb and Dee?"

"The very same."

"That's brilliant!" Her face grew excited. "My girlfriend and I think that's a very romantic inscription. We have a theory that every inscription leaves a lot out—a secret that's hidden between the lines."

Naturally, I was curious. "What's your theory about <u>us</u>?"

"Well," she said, "we decided that you guys were married, but not to each other. But you were in love with each other and had a passionate affair every summer, like the couple in *Same Time, Next Year.*"

When I told her the truth, she decided <u>their</u> story was more dramatic, but <u>ours</u> was better.

Then she said, "I won't keep you any longer. I'm sure you want to get to your bench. It's over there at the end of the row."

I thanked her for her help, said goodbye, and walked quickly toward the bench she'd pointed at.

It was easy to imagine that Dee was already there, waiting for me.

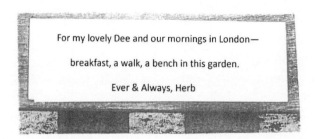

For my lovely Dee and our mornings in London—

breakfast, a walk, a bench in this garden.

Ever & Always, Herb

Plaque and benches in Berkeley Square

May 2

At Home Near the Water

When I returned to Connecticut, I showed Marc the photo of Dee's bench.

"It's really nice," he said. "It's a shame it's so far away. If it were here in Westport, we could stop by any time. And so could the boys."

An hour later, we'd decided to put a plaque on Dee's favorite bench in Westport, the one above Compo Beach across the street from Elvira's Market, where she liked to meet with teachers and friends or sit with me at sunset and look out over the Long Island Sound.

"And what'll the plaque say?" Dee asked.

"We decided to keep it simple. It'll just say:

In Loving Memory of Dee Appleman
Who Always Felt at Home
Near the Water"

"I like that."

May 12

Mother's Day

Early this morning, I sat on Dee's bench and looked out at the Sound. In the distance, I saw waves forming, then cresting, then breaking, until they finally landed on the beach a few yards from me.

Each wave brought a memory. Most were typical memories of motherhood—bathing a baby in a bassinet, taking an anxious little boy to get his first haircut—but a few were special and justified Marc's words at Dee's memorial service: "She was the best."

When Marc was in high school.
During basketball practice, Marc and a teammate dove after a loose ball. The teammate's head crashed into Marc's nose. The coach stopped practice and took Marc to the hospital.

I was out of town, so Dee handled this emergency by herself. As she later reported the incident, "I told him his nose was pushed way off to the side of his face, but he was in denial."

"I know it looks bad," he said, "but don't worry, the doc'll just snap it back into place."

I leaned over, kissed him on the forehead, and said, "No, Marc, your nose is broken. You need surgery."

He insisted he didn't.

"Okay," I said, "if you want to live with a nose that's permanently connected to your left ear.

"The operation went very well. But of course when he came home, his face was swollen and crisscrossed with bandages.

"Your mother stopped by to see him, took one look, and almost fainted. 'This should be a warning, Markey boy. No more basketball. Next time, you could lose an eye.'

"I took her aside and reminded her that Marc loved to play basketball and had worked hard to make the team. Then I said, 'I think it would be wrong to make him give up something he loves just because he might get hurt. It's our job to help him be brave, not scared.'

"She quickly backed down. 'All right, Deedarling, if you say so.' Then with a sigh of regret, she added, 'You should've been my mother. Then maybe I'd be brave too.'"

When Marc was in college.

During our first stay in England, when Wilfrid Hyde White starred in a national tour of *A Perfect Gentleman* and Marc was in a summer program at Oxford, Dee filled her sketchbook with pen-and-ink drawings of London, the English countryside, and a tapestry of English place-names that I thought was the finest calligraphic design she'd ever done.

Marc loved the drawings and offered to have them printed up in a booklet. Although the printing costs were relatively modest, it would take every penny he'd saved from birthday presents and odd jobs, and he'd empty the bank account he'd built up patiently over several years.

I think most mothers would've said, "Oh, no, I can't let you spend all your savings on me." But Dee knew how to accept a compliment and a gift.

"Remember, Dee," her mother had advised her, "when a young man brings you flowers, don't say, 'Oh, you shouldn't have!' Instead, accept them graciously and say, 'Why, thank you! They're lovely!'"

To make sure there was no misunderstanding, her mother added, "I'm not saying you should be insincere. I'm saying you should be grateful."

Which is why Dee accepted Marc's offer without hesitation. "Oh, Marc," she said, "That's so generous of you! And shows such respect for my talent! Thank you! Very much!"

Marc grew four inches taller on the spot!

A calligraphic design of English place-names

A Note on Dee's Calligraphic Design
of English Place-Names

Like an Irving Berlin song that sounds so natural and simple it seems to have written itself, Dee's design looks so unplanned, it's easy to believe that she had nothing to do with it and the words fell into place by themselves.

True, the final design is pleasing to the eye and forms a subtle pattern of interrelated lines, curves, capital letters, small letters, and white spaces that allow the design to breathe—but to most viewers, this seems just a happy accident.

In fact, like Irving Berlin, who was a meticulous craftsman, Dee prepared for this "unplanned" work with a dozen practice sketches and didn't consider her job done until—on the third try—she completed a final design that wasn't marred by even one slip of her calligrapher's pen.

Marc, at forty-two, when Dee was diagnosed with an advanced stage of ovarian cancer.

Marc was an executive at a start-up in California, but he pulled up stakes and brought the family back to Westport, Connecticut, so that everyone could be there for Dee.

For the next two years, during her ups and downs, remissions and recurrences, and until the day she died, he stayed close by, using the time to build a new house, involving Dee every step of the way, showing her the architectural drawings and decoration plans, asking for her input, and giving her something creative to be involved in and something positive to look forward to. In a feat of magic worthy of Dee herself, he turned feelings of love into acts of love every day for two years.

Dee believed the best way to hold on to a grown son was to let him go. After Marc graduated from the University of Michigan and took an apartment near us, she thought we should urge him to leave the Midwest.

"Why?" I asked. "I like having him around. I like the three of us doing things together—watching Tiger games on TV, going to shows and movies, having Sunday brunch…"

"I know. I like it too."

"And so does Marc."

"I'm sure he does. But is it good for him?"

"What're you getting at?"

She spoke slowly, pausing and thinking aloud. "Marc's an only child, and the three of us have always been very close. But that kind of closeness has drawbacks. For Marc, I mean. Because if you're an only child and your parents have strong personalities—which we do—then it's hard to break away. And it's doubly hard if you stay in the nest or even hang around nearby."

As usual, she made a good case. "What do you propose?"

"That we push him out of the nest and let him fly to a place where people don't know him as our son and where, over the next few years, he can become an adult with his own identity."

That night, we talked to him. Dee did most of the talking, unafraid to play the bad guy, confident that whatever she said or did, Marc would know it was said and done out of love.

Later that year, he left for San Diego—a place that was far from the Midwest, where the weather was perfect and the girls were tanned and California-gorgeous. There, he followed his bliss, got a job on a local paper, was quickly offered a better job by the *L.A. Times*, and began to live out his dream of being a sportswriter.

Dee's intuition had been sound. We let him go out of love. And when we needed him most, he came back out of love.

Marc in San Diego

May 13

When Dee Criticized You, You Thanked Her

Reading over yesterday's entries, I was reminded that Dee's love was often tough love. Usually, that kind of love makes the person receiving it defensive or even angry. But when Dee criticized you, you thanked her. As Ira Gershwin said, "Nice work, if you can get it." That certainly never happened to me.

But it routinely happened to Dee. Her secret? Most criticism makes you feel smaller; Dee's made you feel bigger. She reminded you of your better self.

But even I was astounded when we visited my mother in the hospital and Dee—gently but unflinchingly—told Mom, "You should really be more grateful."

There was an unwritten rule in our family: never criticize Mom, never confront her, and always tiptoe around her feelings. Dee had just broken that rule. Now she explained why. "Your recovery is coming along on schedule. You're no longer in pain. You have children who love you and come to visit every day. You should be chirping like a bird. But all you do is complain about the food, the nurses, the other patients, everything."

Mom was shaken but—a rare accomplishment for her—managed to speak up and defend herself. "You know why I complain? Because I'm not in Prospect Park on a picnic. I'm in the Coney Island Hospital, and here, there's a lot to complain about."

Dee wasn't buying it. "There's even more to be grateful for. Three months ago, you had a tracheotomy, and the doctors didn't expect you to live. But you fooled them, you pulled through, and soon you'll be going home."

Mom looked up in the general direction of heaven. "Dear God, can You believe this? I'm in the Coney Island Hospital with a tube down my throat, and they want me to chirp like a bird!"

Dee and I cracked up. "That just proves my point," Dee said. "You can enjoy yourself, and you should! When people visit you, they're worried. You have an obligation to let them see how much better you feel. Instead of complaining, you should show them—"

"How chirpy I can be?"

"Yes!"

As we were leaving, Mom took Dee aside. "You're right, darling. I have a lot to be grateful for. Thank you for reminding me."

Dee kissed her on the cheek. "You're very welcome."

June 16

Father's Day

On Father's Day, Dee served me breakfast in bed; and on the edge of the tray, there was always a beautifully wrapped gift. Looking back, one Father's Day blurs into another—except for 1972, which stands alone in isolated splendor, because in 1972, Dee's gift made me shout, "Hallelujah!"

The gift was a book so new that it hadn't yet been published in America and had to be ordered from Blackwell's in Oxford. The author, who felt the need to write under the pseudonym Alex Comfort, was an English physician and biologist. The title of his book: *The Joy of Sex.*

Here's the letter that came with the book:

> To my darling Herb,
>
> I'm convinced that family happiness has no stronger ally than a good marriage, and a good marriage has no stronger ally than sexual happiness.
> Of course it takes love to create sexual happiness— but it also takes skill and understanding. I think this book will enhance our skill and understanding.
> As a bonus, the text is illustrated with drawings that are both instructive and beautiful.
> Now comes the juicy part!
> I don't think we should use this book as a reference work that we consult now and then. Instead, I think we should read a page a night and turn The Joy of Sex into a year-long workshop and adventure.
> What do you say?
>
> Happy Father's Day and All My Love,
> Dee

Are you kidding? I said, "Hallelujah!" (Actually, I <u>shouted</u> it!)

*　　*　　*

Summary of our year-end report:

Forty percent of the acts described in *The Joy of Sex*, we didn't bother to finish.

Forty percent we <u>did</u> finish—but only once.

Twenty percent we liked very much and incorporated into our lovemaking from then on.

June 17

Sexy Secretaries

The Joy of Sex encouraged us to venture into other forbidden territories.

"It all started," Dee remembered, "because the women at the beauty parlor whispered and giggled and made a big fuss about porno flicks. I became curious and asked you to rent one. Then it slipped my mind until I went into Blockbuster one night to pick up a new movie. As I was checking it out, the guy behind the counter said, 'Just to remind you, *Sexy Secretaries* is overdue.' I gave him a blank stare. 'You're Appleman, right? Well, *Sexy Secretaries* was checked out to your name, and it's overdue.' When I came back to the car, I demanded to know, 'What's going on with *Sexy Secretaries?*'"

"Hey," I laughed. "didn't you say you wanted to rent a porno flick?"

"Yes, but—"

"Okay, I rented one."

Without another word, we went straight home and put the video on. After about ten minutes, Dee turned it off. Then she said something that surprised me. "I'm <u>so</u> glad I saw that!"

"Why?"

"Because," she said slyly, "it's always good to know what the competition is up to." Then she corrected herself. "No, it's because I was curious. And I'll admit my curiosity was rewarded. The sight of a handsome naked man and a beautiful naked woman having sex and giving each other pleasure was exciting. I'd be a hypocrite to deny it."

After a moment's thought, she added. "Having said that, I also have to say pornography has a problem—a little goes a long way. Looking at a naked couple who never talk gets boring pretty quickly."

Still, she was grateful to *Sexy Secretaries* for reminding us that although sex might end in the bedroom, it didn't begin there. "It begins hours before when we walk along the beach and talk, or go for a drive in the country and listen to a cassette that fills the car with Mozart, or when I'm getting dinner ready and you come into the kitchen just to touch me, or you're stretched out on the sofa, reading, and I lean over to kiss you. The bedroom is our destination, but getting there is half the fun.'"

And once we got there, that wasn't always the end of the story. Making love often made us hungry and sent us into the kitchen to raid the icebox, snack on cold chicken and white wine, then return to bed, cuddle in the spoon position, and treat ourselves to an old movie.

Recalling some of our favorite after-sex movies, we decided that our all-time favorite was *The Story of Vernon and Irene Castle*, the last of the black-and-white musicals starring Fred Astaire and Ginger Rogers. We liked that one best because all their other black-and-white musicals were screwball comedies about <u>falling</u> in love, while *The Story of Vernon and Irene Castle*, based on the true story of the Castles, was about <u>married</u> love. And we always thought <u>married</u> love was more interesting—and more romantic—and, done right, sexier.

July 3

Midnight Swim

Today is Dee's birthday. She would've been sixty-eight today.

MEMORIES OF MAKING LOVE #4

The Night Dee Turned Fifty

Dee had been okay with turning thirty and even forty, but turning fifty was crossing into AARP territory. "From now on," she sighed, "the kindest compliment I can expect is 'She looks young . . . for her age.'"

Clearly, she was feeling very sorry for herself. She wouldn't let me buy her a special present or make a party or even invite friends to join us for dinner. All she wanted to do was have a quiet meal in a neighborhood restaurant and then go straight home.

When we got home (it wasn't even nine), she quickly undressed and went to bed. But she couldn't fall asleep.

She was still awake at midnight.

That's when I got on my white horse and rode to the rescue. We were living in a lovely garden apartment in Troy, Michigan. I suggested we go for a swim, figuring that she needed some exercise to tire her out.

"No," she said, "I don't feel like it. Besides, the pool is closed."

"So? We'll climb over the fence. It's dark. No one'll see us."

Reluctantly, she agreed, and we walked to the pool. Then I gave her a hand up, and she climbed over the fence. A second later, I followed.

The night was balmy, and the midnight darkness was seductive. "Hey," I said, "why don't we go skinny dipping?"

Dee smiled wryly. "You're determined to salvage this birthday, aren't you?"

"Not at all," I said. "It's just that I was brought up to be kind to old ladies."

She stuck out her tongue at me.

Then we swam and splashed each other and kissed (kissing is very underrated) and came out of the pool and spread our towels.

And the next thing I knew, it was almost dawn, and I woke up to find Dee drying her hair and humming.

"You seem happy," I said.

"Why shouldn't I be? Last night, on my fiftieth birthday, I went skinny dipping with my husband. And we swam and made love, just as if we were still twenty."

Then, returning to the present, she became very serious.

"Last summer, as I faced up to the fact that I was probably going to die soon, I did a lot of thinking. Inevitably, I had second thoughts about this choice or that choice, but I had no second thoughts about us. Sometimes I was overcome by sadness, but never by regret." Then she corrected herself. "No, that's not true. I had <u>one</u> regret. That I wouldn't be around when you win your Tony Award and your Olivier Award!"

"I'm afraid that's a fantasy."

"I know. That's why when it happens, they'll say it's <u>fantastic</u>!"

July 5

Other, Deeper Regrets

I woke up in the middle of the night with a heavy heart because I remembered another regret, a deeper regret, that Dee had chosen not to mention—a regret for the second child we'd never had.

Though we came awfully close.

When Dee became pregnant at the age of thirty-two, she was so happy she made jokes about morning sickness. She became even happier when she found out that she was carrying a girl. The prospect of having a daughter enchanted her. Then halfway through her pregnancy, she came down with german measles and suffered a miscarriage within a week.

Her gynecologist explained that nature had done us a favor because the baby surely would've had a serious birth defect. Dee's conscious mind agreed with him, but that didn't keep her from becoming blue and staying blue for several months.

Still the door wasn't permanently closed. Dee was relatively young, and though her biological clock was ticking, it was ticking slowly.

And indeed, a year later, she became pregnant again. Then in her third month, she slipped and fell down the last few steps of a staircase in the Frick Museum, landing hard on her belly and side.

I rushed her by taxi to Mount Sinai, the nearest hospital, twenty blocks north of the Frick. When the emergency room doctor examined her, he confirmed what she already knew—she'd lost the baby.

This second loss took the heart out of her. She didn't want to try again. Characteristically, she never said a word about what might've been, the family we might've had. But that silence said a lot.

* * *

This afternoon's mail brought a letter from the town of Westport that helped me replace those old regrets with the gladness of anticipation. The letter read, *"We are pleased to inform you that your plaque in memory of Dee Appleman has been installed on the bench that you designated."*

July 6

A Bench along Compo Beach

Early the next morning, Marc and I went down to Compo Beach to have a look at Dee's plaque. When we got there, a young woman was sitting on the bench, keeping an eye on two little girls who were playing in the sand. I asked her how she happened to be sitting on this particular bench. "Well," she said, "I noticed the new plaque, and when I saw it was dedicated to Dee Appleman, I thought how nice it would be to sit here and remember her."

"Oh," I asked, "did you know Dee?"

She nodded. "My girls went to A Child's Place, where Dee was the executive director. We all thought she was very special." Then she turned to face me, suddenly curious. "Did <u>you</u> know her?"

In my head, I heard Dee say, "Yes, he did. In fact, almost every night, he sang to me."

Plaque and bench in Westport

August 29

Her Last Notebook

Today was the first anniversary of Dee's death.

I wandered through the house aimlessly. Then my feet led me to the little bookcase where Dee had kept her notebooks and sketchbooks. I pulled out her last notebook and began to leaf through it. Unlike her notebooks from cruises and trips abroad, which were specific to those experiences, this notebook just had two unrelated entries.

The Time I Felt Like Lucille Ball

The cancer was acting up today, and so to cheer myself up, I thought of the funniest thing I'd ever done.

We were at a tennis resort. On the last morning of our stay, the head pro set up a match between the two most improved players—Herb and Hank.

Hank's wife, Vicki, and the rest of our group watched from a wooden grandstand at the side of the court.

The guys played hard, but didn't knock themselves out—it was a fun match. Or so I thought until Vicki jumped up, pointed her finger at Herb, and screamed, "Foot fault! Foot fault!"

This was so inappropriate, so overly competitive, that everyone was embarrassed.

I don't know what came over me, but suddenly I jumped up too and screamed, "Call the tennis police! Call the tennis police!"

The laughter came in waves—the first wave stopped, and the second started, then the second stopped, and the third wave started.

And I felt like Lucille Ball!

A Bread-and-Butter Letter

When I was a little girl and had just learned to print, my mother told me that, as soon as I came home from a playdate or party, I had to write the hostess a bread-and-butter letter, thanking her for making the playdate or party so nice.

When you leaf through my last notebook, as I know you will, this bread-and-butter letter will be waiting for you.

To my darling Herb,

On my seventeenth birthday, I drew up a wish list about the man I wanted to marry. I wished for someone who'd be a handsome and passionate lover; a wonderful father; a talented man who'd earn a good living doing work I admired; and a best friend who'd encourage me in <u>my</u> work.

He'd also be someone who made literature, history, art, music, and theater part of our daily life, and who saw to it that Shakespeare, Rembrandt, Mozart, and many of the other great men and women who created civilization, were frequent visitors to our home, and that we often visited <u>them,</u> in theaters, museums, concert halls, and on sightseeing trips abroad.

Above all, he'd realize that everything we lived through, in fact or imagination, would never be complete until we talked about it.

I don't think there are many women who, looking back over a lifetime, can put a check next to every box on the wish list they wrote when they were seventeen.

But I can. So this bread-and-butter letter is my thank-you for making all the playdates and parties of our marriage an endless number of "nice" experiences— although "nice" is a very small word for the gift of a fulfilled life.

Darling--
We've had fifty years--
not only of time together,
but of sharing a conversation
that was everything I'd hoped for—
and a love that was more than I'd hoped for.

Ever & always,
Dee

PS And God saw that it was not good for Man to be alone, so He created Eve. Don't mourn too long. Give yourself a chance to find a new Eve.

The Next Three Months

September 10

Trying to Find Someone

In casual conversation, I let a few old friends know I was ready to meet someone. Each man said, "Good idea," and went back to watching television. But each woman heard my news as a call to action and immediately began flipping through the Rolodex in her head. Only women, it seems, have a matchmaking gene.

Soon, I was invited to a dinner party where Phyllis, a widow, was seated next to me. Several days later, I was invited to a cocktail party where, the moment I arrived, I was guided across the room to meet Ellen, a divorced woman.

(Phyllis and Ellen aren't their real names; throughout, I've changed the names of the women I've met to protect their privacy.)

It was immediately obvious that my friends and I had different ideas about the right woman for me. They were offering me a companion, but I didn't want a companion. I wanted a new partner for romance, sex, and love.

And something else was obvious: my friends had introduced me to women my own age. But the sight of these women did not quicken my pulse.

Such a thought, I knew, was politically incorrect and lacking in gallantry; nevertheless, when I spoke to other men my age, I found that most of them felt the same way. To prove how natural and widespread our feelings were, one man even showed me a list of famous May-December marriages that he'd put together.

Famous May-December Marriages
with Ages of Husband and Wife
at Time of Marriage

Pablo Casals	80
Marta (wife)	21
Age difference	59
Fred Astaire	81
Robyn (wife)	35
Age difference	46
Pablo Picasso	80
Jacqueline (wife)	34
Age difference	46
Charlie Chaplin	54
Oona (wife)	18
Age difference	36
Bing Crosby	54
Kathy (wife)	23
Age difference	31
Humphrey Bogart	45
Lauren (wife)	20
Age difference	25

Dee chuckled, conceding my point; then she picked up the list of May-December marriages and reviewed the various age differentials. "So who do you want to be? Casals, with a Marta who was fifty-nine years younger than he was? Picasso, with a Jacqueline who was forty-six years younger? Bogart, with a Lauren Bacall who was twenty-five years younger?"

"I don't know." I said, holding my palms up in a gesture of confusion. "If it isn't too awkward, I'd like your advice."

That tickled her. "What makes you think it'll be the advice you want to hear?"

"It usually was," I said. "Still, I'll understand if you pass. It's a bizarre situation."

"It certainly is!" Then she sighed, gave in, thought for a moment, and said, "I hate to be a killjoy, but I don't think a girl in her twenties would be right for you."

I pretended to be disappointed. "How can you say that?"

"She wouldn't know any Rodgers and Hart songs."

"Good point."

"And if she loved you, she'd want to have a baby."

She paused, thought again, and said, "For the same reason, a woman in her thirties or early forties wouldn't be right either. She'd still be young enough to want a baby. And a woman in her late forties or early fifties would probably have children living at home, and you'd have to be their stepfather. Knowing you, that's a responsibility you'd take seriously. Too seriously. It'd become a full-time job."

"So who's left?"

She looked at me with a straight face. "A woman of ninety?" Then she giggled. "No, strike that. Who's left is someone in her late fifties or early sixties—"

"But looks younger—"

"You're incorrigible!"

"I'm also determined. This time, I won't rely on friends to fix me up. I'll look on my own."

September 12

Phone Call

But look <u>where?</u>

I decided to try the personal ads in my alumni magazines.

… One ad seemed particularly promising. The woman was a book editor, lived in Boston, was fifty-three years old, and in her own modest opinion, was "still pretty enough to turn heads." Should I write and ask for a photo? Or should I call and hear what she sounded like?

I called.

"Hi," I said. "I'm answering your ad. I want my head turned."

She laughed. "I'll see what I can do." Her voice was low, smoky, and appealing.

"My name is Herb," I said.

"How do you do, Herb? My name is Louise."

"I'm widowed," I said, "after a long happy marriage, and I'm just starting to reach out."

"I'm widowed too," she said. "And I've been reaching out for several years. It isn't easy."

…Pause, as we begin the ritual of getting to know each other.

"Do you have a family, Herb?"

"Yes. A son and two grandsons. And you?"

"Two daughters. But no grandchildren—yet."

Another pause, as we shift gears.

"Did your wife have a career?"

"Yes, she did. She was the headmistress of a private elementary school, an artist who illustrated several books, and a published author."

"She sounds remarkable."

"She was. In fact, she was the most remarkable person I've ever known."

When I told Dee what I'd said, she shook her head. "No, don't go there. I know you love me and always will. But when you talk to another woman, keep me out of it. Give the lady a chance. Don't make her feel that she's competing with a saint." Then she sang the intro to an old comedy number, a neglected gem that the cabaret singer Andrea Marcovicci had rediscovered:

> *There once lived a wonderful woman,*
> *A marvelous woman was she*
> *She cooked like an angel,*
> *Made all her own clothes,*
> *At four every morning this paragon rose--*
> *She was my husband's first wife!*

"I'm afraid it's too late," I said. "I <u>did</u> talk about you. At length."

"You shouldn't have. We have a past no one can touch. But the present and future should be reserved for someone else." Then she asked, "Did you make a date?"

"Uh-huh," I said, "for lunch on Saturday. We're going to meet halfway between Boston and Redding—in Hartford. At the restaurant in the Wadsworth Atheneum."

"Bon appétit!"

September 14

Rendezvous in Hartford

I got to the restaurant early. When Louise walked in, I knew my head <u>wouldn't</u> be turned.

Dee was puzzled. "How could you know so quickly?"

"I just did. It doesn't take a man long to know if he thinks a woman is desirable." Then I continued, adding an asterisk to my last remark, "Of course, sex is just the foundation. To build the rest of the house and make it livable, you have to share the same values, get enthusiastic about the same things, show each other kindness, and ultimately fall in love. But sex is the foundation. That has to come first."

Dee felt that a woman's house was built on a different foundation. "A woman is programmed to want a man who can take good care of her and her children. That means she needs to get to know him and assess his character, which takes a while. And though sex matters to her too, she can wait and let it develop gradually."

The rumor, it seems, is true: men and women are different.

Louise and I sat in the restaurant, making small talk, letting the scene play itself out. After lunch, we walked around the museum and viewed several exhibits. Then, having observed the courtesies, we pecked each other on the cheek and said goodbye.

I turned to go, but she lingered. "Will you call me?" she asked.

I didn't want to be unkind, but I didn't want to mislead her. "Look," I said, "we both knew this was a long shot, and long shots, by definition, rarely win."

She shrugged. "At least you're honest."

I shrugged. "As you said on the phone, it isn't easy being single again."

On the drive back to Redding, I decided that rather than answer one ad at a time, I'd place my own ad; if I got seven or eight responses, I'd have better odds of finding someone.

September 18

Cary Seeks Deborah

I placed my ad in the personal columns of the Sunday edition of the *New York Times*, an edition that covered the Tri State area of New York, New Jersey, and Connecticut. This coverage guaranteed that the women would live nearby, and it would be convenient for us to get together. The ad ran today. The top line, in capitals and boldface type, read, CARY SEEKS DEBORAH.

Dee chuckled. "That'll get a girl's attention."

The reference, of course, was to Cary Grant and Deborah Kerr, who costarred in *An Affair to Remember*. To many fans, they were as romantic as any lovers in movie history—witty, glamorous, tender, ardent, separated by accident, and reunited by love.

Below the top line, in regular type, the ad continued, "Widowed after a long happy marriage."

"Another plus," Dee said. "It shows you aren't a bachelor who doesn't know how to live with a woman or a divorced man who resents women."

Then after a few words about what I did for a living, I ended by saying, "I'm looking for romance and love with—think Deborah Kerr in *An Affair to Remember*. You're looking for same with—think Cary Grant in *An Affair to Remember*. If we're going to dream, we may as well dream big."

"Okay," Dee sighed, "where do I sign up?"

To get in touch with me, they were instructed to call a general number, punch in my code, and listen to this recorded message:"If you find my ad appealing, please leave your number, and I'll call you."

Dee predicted the phone would ring off the hook.

September 20

Would You Believe?

And she was right! In four days, I received more than seventy calls.

"My God," Dee said, in mock alarm. "How did you survive?"

"I called everyone who left a message, told them the response to my ad had been overwhelming, and explained that, to cut the number down to a manageable size, I was asking each woman for a photo."

"Did any of them object?"

I nodded. "Twelve. They didn't want to be judged on such a superficial basis. I sympathized with them but insisted, and they dropped out. To the rest, I promised that if I felt the chemistry was right, I'd call and offer to send my photo."

"Which one?"

"I never had to choose. They all said they could tell from my ad and my voice that I was worth a cup of coffee."

In the end, I arranged to meet nine of them.

September 23

From Oscar's to Ferraro's to Oscar's

We met in the city over the next three days. Since it's almost a four-hour round-trip from Redding to mid-Manhattan, I scheduled three meetings a day. It would've worn me out to drive in more often.

I started, at one, with lunch at Oscar's, the restaurant in the Waldorf Astoria; then, at three, I had coffee at Ferraro's, the little Italian take-out place on Madison Avenue; then, at five, I went back to Oscar's for cocktails. I figured that even if someone came early or stayed late, she wouldn't see me with someone else.

Dee was impressed. "Ike could've used you on D-Day."

"It was very interesting," I said. "First of all, these women were relatively young. The youngest was forty-four, the oldest fifty-six, and most were around fifty. And from what I could tell, they didn't seem to care that I was considerably older."

"Why should they? You don't <u>look</u> old or <u>act</u> old. And in some ways, your age works to their advantage."

"Really?"

"Do the arithmetic. Say the woman is fifty. A man her own age is dating other women who are thirty-something or even twenty-something. To him, she's relatively old. But to you, she's still young. Also, a man her own age is at the peak of his career with an overcrowded schedule. But you have time for her—time to drop into a museum or linger over coffee or go for a walk on a weekday afternoon. And don't forget the travel. A man her own age, even if he can afford to take her on a cruise —and if he's paying alimony and child support, that's a big if—it's not easy for him to get away for a week or two."

"Maybe you're right," I said. "Anyhow, whatever the reason, age wasn't a factor for me or for them."

"So," Dee said, "there were nine contestants and they were all relatively young and nice—"

"But not nice enough."

"Not even <u>one</u>?"

I paused, cleared my throat, and to an imaginary roll of drums, made my announcement. "Yes," I said, "there is <u>one</u>." And then I filled in the details.

Her name is Rita. She's fifty-seven and quite attractive, though not at all like Deborah Kerr. She's been around the block, doesn't kid herself, and has a look that says, "What the hell, why not?" She was married eight years but never had children. She's been divorced twelve years, has had a successful career, and is now senior vice president at a top ad agency. Still, she isn't my type, and I didn't encourage her. But she didn't need encouragement. We were shaking hands, bidding each other goodbye, when all of a sudden, she said, "Listen, I have a proposition—"

I smiled. "You sure that's the word you want?"

"Yes," she said, "that's exactly the word I want."

"Then we better sit down again."

And sure enough, she propositioned me. "It's obvious," she said, "that with Dee you had the whole package and that for you, I'm not the whole package. But look, until the whole package comes along, I think I can be a nice stopgap." I asked her what exactly she had in mind.

"My proposition," she said, "is that we get together once or twice a week for friendly sex."

I repeated the phrase, not sure I'd heard her right. "Is such a thing possible?"

"Oh yes," she assured me. "It isn't love or marriage or even living together. It's just a way of being friendly, of going on a date once or twice a week, but with this difference—we'll skip dinner and the movies. We'll just have sex. It won't be like *For Whom the Bell Tolls*. We won't be in a sleeping bag in Spain."

"And the earth won't move."

"Agreed. But on the plus side, you'll feel that you're a man, I'll feel that I'm a woman, and afterward, we'll both feel relaxed." Then, without the least hesitation or embarrassment, she said, "Since we've already had two drinks and I live only a few blocks from here, why don't we go to my apartment?"

Dee finally spoke up. "Don't tell me anymore. It'll be awkward and make you feel guilty. Besides, it doesn't concern me. You're single, and you have every right to act single."

Which I did.

October 29

A Short Run

That was the start of my "friendship" with Rita. We usually met twice a week, and our meetings proved that if a man and woman are very lonely and reasonably attractive, it's easy for them to wind up in bed together.

But what began as a physical experience between two bodies soon became an emotional experience between two people. And when that happened, our "friendship" was put to the test.

"In what way?"

"A relationship isn't static—either it becomes more satisfying or else it becomes stale and a burden."

Dee nodded her understanding. "And yours--?"

"Failed the test."

"Why?"

"It's an old story—sex with love is joy; sex without love is exercise."

Last night, after a short run, my "friendship" with Rita closed.

November 19

Dinner Introductions

I let two weeks go by, then tried again, prompted by a commercial on WQXR.

The advertiser was Dinner Introductions, and their pitch was, "We carefully screen eight strangers—four men and four women, all over the age of forty; then we arrange for them to have dinner together. It's like a blind date, except you have four chances instead of one, and you have seven helpers to keep the conversation going."

Dee was all for it. "I think you should call them."

I did. They were very professional. A trained psychologist led me through an in-depth interview that clarified what I felt I <u>had</u> to have and what I was willing to be flexible about.

"So you had dinner?" Dee asked.

"I had <u>three</u> dinners and met <u>twelve</u> women. But if there were bells in the air, I never heard them."

"Never mind," Dee assured me. "The odds are, if you've been happily married once—"

"No," I interrupted, "that's a myth. From what I've seen, a man who was happily married and finds someone else is either very lucky or has very modest expectations. But I was married to <u>you</u>, so I have <u>great</u> expectations."

"Nevertheless," Dee insisted, "there <u>has</u> to be someone. And one day, you'll bump into her."

"Where?"

"Wherever she's waiting for you."

Epilogue

The Olivier Awards

In 2005, *Dauntless Dick Deadeye*, my new version of *HMS Pinafore*, was offered to the Open Air Theatre in London.

Luckily for me, Ian Talbot, the artistic director of the Open Air, really liked what I'd done and offered to produce *Deadeye* that summer. When we met in his office in Regent's Park, he told me, "I hope you realize, this isn't the first revision of *Pinafore* that's come my way. But the others were merely stunts. Your version has really been thought through. Not only is your conception damn clever, but your dialogue and lyrics blend perfectly with Gilbert's. I figure you've rewritten about 70 percent of the original, but no one but an expert would ever know it. You've done a beautiful job. And in the process, I think you've actually improved on Gilbert."

The London critics agreed. The *Sunday Times* gave the production four stars and commended Ian Talbot for choosing "Herbert Appleman's version rather than the Savoy Opera original." The *Sunday Telegraph* had a "deliriously happy evening on board the *HMS Pinafore*, thanks to the wonderfully entertaining version by Herbert Appleman." *Stage Online* also expressed thanks for "a libretto that has been extensively revised by Herbert Appleman and thereby rescues a show that has become mired in tradition and (gives) it a fresh and refreshing lick of energy." And the *Guardian* said simply, the show "achieves that touch of ecstasy that is the *sine qua non* of all good musicals."

Dee thought it sounded like a hit!

"It was," I said. "It had enormous crossover appeal. We got the musical theater fans, the Gilbert and Sullivan diehards, families with young children, and sophisticated theatergoers on dates. We even got repeat business—people who came back a second time, bringing friends and relatives with them."

Dauntless Dick Deadeye

Curtain Call led by Queen Victoria as honorary member of cast

Photo Credit: Alastair Muir & Regent's Park Open Air Theatre, London

Dee was glowing. "Surely after that, you transferred to the West End."

"We would have if—"

"If _what_? What happened _this_ time?" And then I told her about the terrorist attacks. "A train in the London underground was bombed, and at the same time, a bus on the street was bombed. Fifty people were killed, and nearly seven hundred were injured."

"Oh no!"

"Of course, tourism was affected and theater attendance, especially in the West End, went down—way down. The producer we'd been negotiating with pulled out. 'This is no time to transfer an expensive musical to the West End.'"

Dee bit her lip to keep from crying.

"By November," I continued, "things were back to normal. But the window of opportunity had closed. By then, our summer run was over, and our cast had dispersed."

"Surely," Dee said, "that can't be the end of the story."

"No, another window opened—slightly. In January, the nominations were announced for the 2006 Olivier Awards. Only two musicals were nominated for Outstanding Musical Production—the West End revival of _Guys and Dolls_ and the Open Air production of _Dauntless Dick Deadeye_.

"I flew over for the Awards ceremony in February, and Marc came with me."

"I'm glad," Dee said. "He's always been there for your big nights."

"It was, of course, a very glamorous occasion. The ceremonies were held in the Grand Ballroom of the London Hilton. Everyone was in evening dress. And every face was flushed with false happiness and real anxiety."

"Please," Dee said, "I can't stand it! Tell me."

"_Guys and Dolls_ won."

"Damn!"

I'd prepared an acceptance speech, but never got to deliver it.

Dee asked if I remembered what I was going to say.

I nodded. "I was going to say, 'I have three thank-you's.

"To Ian Talbot and the Open Air Theatre for giving *Deadeye* a magical production.

"To my son, Marc, who was *Deadeye's* biggest fan.

"And to my late wife, Dee, who always knew this night would come and I'd finally get to eat those damn grapes.'"

Then I explained the grapes allusion, ending with, "Tantalus doesn't get the grapes, but Dee predicted I would—because I was a better writer than Tantalus."

"I realize," Dee admitted, "my prediction hasn't come true. But I refuse to concede. All the returns aren't in yet."

"Okay. I'll treat it like a breaking news story…"

She nodded, smiled, and typed in the words: *More to come…*